PRAY
WIT
CELTIC HOLY
WOMEN

MW00640508

Praying with Celtic holy Women

BRIDGET MARY MEEHAN AND
REGINA MADONNA OLIVER

Liguori/Triumph
LIGUORI, MISSOURI

Imprimi Potest:
Richard Thibodeau, C.Ss.R.
Provincial, Denver Province
The Redemptorists

Published by Liguori/Triumph
An imprint of Liguori Publications
Liguori, Missouri
www.liguori.org
www.catholicbooksonline.com

Library of Congress Cataloging-in-Publication Data

Meehan, Bridget Mary, 1948–
   Praying with Celtic holy women / Bridget Mary Meehan and Regina Madonna Oliver—1st ed.
     p. cm.
   Includes bibliographical references (p. 211)
   ISBN 0-7648-0929-6 (pbk.)
   1. Christian saints, Celtic—British Isles. 2. Christian women saints— British Isles. 3. Spirituality—Celtic Church. I. Oliver, Regina Madonna, 1931– II. Title.

BR754.A1 M44 2003
274.1'0092'3916—dc21   .   2002034104

Printed in Canada
07 06 05 04 03   5 4 3 2 1
First edition

Dedication

To my mother, Bridie Meehan, whose fondness for Mary and the Irish saints reflected a deep faith that heaven is indeed always ready to help us. She now rests in their eternal embrace and is but a prayer away. My father, Jack, whose enchanted stories of fairies, banshees, rabbits, and badgers introduced me to the richness of the mystical magic of the Celtic spirit. I treasure his warmth and companionship. My Aunt Molly McCarthy, whose gentle spirit will live forever in my heart. My brothers, Sean and Patrick, my sisters-in-law, Nancy and Valerie; and my niece and nephew, Katie and Danny, who are special blessings in my life.

To all my Irish relatives who exemplify the wisdom and wit of the Celtic tradition: my grandparents: Bridget Neary and Pat Beale, Katie Doyle and John Meehan. My aunts: Peg Meehan, Tess Murphy, and Kathleen McNamara. My cousins: Aidan and Margaret Ryan, Noreen and Ger Davy, Mary D. and John Meehan, Mary and Bernie Ferns, Pat and Eileen Meehan, Seamus Meehan, Esther Meehan, Kate and Lizzie Murphy, Mary Tregent, Eileen Meehan and Eileen Preston, Alice and Sean Meehan, and Tim and Rose Meehan. Aidan shared with us one of our primary sources on Saint Ita. Aidan and Margaret drove us across Ireland to catch the ferry to Wales. We are grateful for Noreen and Ger Davy and Margaret and Aidan Ryan who opened their homes to us and helped us in our research for this book. Joe Davy conducted a pilgrimage to Saint Brigit's Rock, a sacred site in Ballybuggy, Rathdowney, County Laois.

–Bridget Mary Meehan

I dedicate this book to the many women in my life who, whether of Irish ancestry or not, have demonstrated in their lives the virtues of the holy women we commemorate here. The saints in our book have often been the initiators and builders, not just of monasteries, but of growing Christian communities. So many of the women I name in this dedication are builders, today, here on Chincoteague and elsewhere, of loving Christian communities. For their inspiration, support, and friendship, I thank the following: Eva Mummert, Joan Palmer, Eva Walsh, Kathryn Nee, Mary Pauls, Marg Amrien, Carol Franz, Anne Stephenson, Mary Meehan, Pauline Hoppe, Karen Ramage, Carol Jacob, Anne Hollinger, Dawn Birch, Irma Birch, Darlene Cherrix, Tesha Lewia, Emily Brothers, Kay Welsh, Sarah Muenster, Darlene Spurlock, Doris Schlesinger, Jane Dunn, Susan Gordon, Irene Manning, Alba Thompson, Toni Meunier, Virginia Limon, Nancy Healy, and Diane Weymouth. I also thank, for their support, the women of our family: Diane Oliver, Sylvia Ho Oliver, Barbara Oliver Forth, Ellen Oliver and Carol Oliver, who are carrying the torch in this present generation as they shape the upcoming one! May we continue to follow our unique call and seek "the place of our resurrection"! Like Ita, may we teach the young; like Cannera, may we stand up for the dignity of women; like Gobnait, may we be compassionate and forceful community members; like Brigit, may we put the needs of others foremost; like Dymphna, may we flee from evil; like Hilda, may we nurture giftedness wherever we find it, and like all the Holy Women may we continue to be women who shape our generation in Christian values!

–Regina Madonna Oliver

Contents

Introduction ix

PART I
HEALING WELLS:
SPRINGS OF CELTIC SPIRITUALITY 1

1. The Celtic Soul 3
2. Celtic Holy Women: Our Sacred Guides and
    Companions 11
3. A Celtic Spiritual Adventure 17

PART II
CELTIC HOLY WOMEN OF IRELAND 21

4. Saint Brigit of Kildare: A Reflection of God's Mercy 23
5. Saint Ita of Killeedy: Foster Mother of the Saints of
    Ireland 39
6. Saint Monenna of Killeevy: Intercessor for Peace 51
7. Saint Cannera of Bantry Bay: Patron of Celtic
    Persistence 61
8. Saint Gobnait of Ballyvourney: God-Seeker and
    Pursuer of Justice 71
9. Saint Dymphna of Achill Island: Survivor & Healer 83
10. Saint Samthann of Clonbroney: Wise Soul Friend 97
11. Mary of Nazareth: Our Blessed Mother 107

PART III
PIONEER SAINTS OF WALES 123

12. Saint Non: Icon of Holy Birthing 125
13. Saint Melangell: Patron of Ecology and Holistic
     Healing 137
14. Saint Winefride: Restored to Life 149
15. Saint Tegla: Promoter of Wellness and Balance 165
16. Saint Dwynwen: Patroness of Lovers and Relationships 175

PART IV
EARLY MISSIONARY SAINTS OF CORNWALL
AND OTHER CELTIC SAINTS 183

17. Saint Hilda of Whitby: Mentor and Teacher 185
18. Saint Ia: Missionary to Cornwall and Bearer
     of God News 195
19. Other Saints of the Celtic Tradition 205
        Saint Innywee: Healer of Warts 205
        Saint Gwen Teirbron: Patroness of Nursing Mothers 206
        Saint Helen Luyddog: Patroness of Travelers 207
        Saint Tannoch: Patroness of Survivors of Violent Crimes 207
        Saint Tydfil: A Herbal Healer 208
        Saint Caitigern: Monastic Founder 209

APPENDICES

Appendix 1:   Annotated Bibliography 211
Appendix 2:   Additional Resources for
               Celtic Sacred Journeys 225
Appendix 3:   Recipes 235
Appendix 4:   A Circle Dance 237
Appendix 5:   Weaving the Brigit Cross 241

Introduction

At this threshold of both hope and anxiety, women are reclaiming wisdom figures from ancient cultures as guides in these times of change and transformation. Holy women in the Celtic Christian community are being rediscovered by twenty-first-century seekers who are interested in integration and wholeness, healing, empowerment, and compassion for all people on the margins.

Our search for the rich legacy of these saints leads us to holy places sacred to their memory. This book invites readers on a journey through Ireland, Wales, and Cornwall where we contemplate the sacred feminine in Celtic spirituality. Here you will connect with the age-old Christian traditions and their sometimes pagan antecedents, discover how springs and holy wells were associated with birthing and healing, and contemplate the feminine wisdom hidden in Celtic traditions. Here you will meet women who were spiritual leaders, prophets, martyrs, and *anam charas* or spiritual friends in the early Celtic Church. Let us invite these women of faith to accompany us in the twenty-first century: that we may "be like Christ" in our generation, as they were in theirs.

We celebrate the lives of our loved ones after their deaths, in pictures, stories, and prayer, and within a generation or two, our families often forget their legacy, and memories grow dim. But what if the memory of a holy person is still celebrated by the community fifteen hundred years after her death through daily prayerful visits to a site, a concerned upkeep of that property, and the continuing reverential use of water from the sainted person's well? Clearly, this centuries-old popularity indicates a life that conveys a universal truth and wisdom across the ages. These soul friends and partners speak inspirationally to us, standing as we do at the cusp of a new millennium.

During our research and study trips to Ireland and Wales, we (Bridget Mary and Regina) sought to connect with the unique women who have continued to impress the people of their communities from ancient times. We have specifically sought out women whose roles and deeds may have been underplayed. We wish to reclaim the lost voices of these women who were powerful religious leaders, so that women of today may connect with them and discover their own spiritual identity.

Our quest for holy women and their healing wells is a pursuit of the feminine spirit, the intuitive insight, the mystical vision, the creation-inspired heart, the generous hospitality, the sense of joy, the holistic approach to life that is found in the richness of Celtic spirituality and culture. So we welcome everyone, regardless of age, culture, gender, or ethnic origin to join us in an adventure of the spirit—our journey to the soul of the Celtic.

In Celtic tradition, the holy feminine is often associated with sacred wells and rivers. According to some estimates, there are about three thousand holy wells in Ireland. Some of the spiritual traditions connected with them were strongly influenced by pre-Christian practices. The Druids believed

that water was life-giving and that wells and springs possessed magical healing properties, often associated with curing specific illnesses. Offerings such as coins and pins have
frequently been found in wells, rivers, and lakes. The Shannon River is associated with the goddess Sinend who would
seek wisdom from the well of Coelrind/Connla, but the well
overtook her and changed her into the river that bears her name.

The author of a book on Celtic pilgrimage sites has observed: "The religious patterns or rounds [used at the holy
wells] usually consisted of recitations of the rosary and repeated circling of the well with the pilgrims perhaps on their
knees performing acts of penance. A longing for healing was
a major motivating factor in such visits to the wells, with the
water being bathed in, drunk, or carried home....Modern
scientific analysis has in many cases shown that the mineral
content of certain wells does indeed contain medicinal qualities and may assist in the healing of certain sicknesses. Typi-
cally, the one seeking healing would leave behind at the well,
tied to a tree or a bush, a small rag torn from his or her
garment, symbolizing the leaving behind of the ailment" (Sister Cintra Pemberton, *Soulfaring*, Harrisburg, Pennsylvania:
Morehouse Publishing, 1999). At several holy wells in both
Ireland and Wales, we noticed symbols left behind by visitors: rags hung on trees at Monenna's well in South Armagh,
coins in Saint Brigit's and Saint Dymphna's well in Ireland,
and flowers at Saint Non's well in Wales.

When Christianity came to Ireland, it did not so much
supplant the culture that the Druidic society had developed,
but rather borrowed from and baptized those characteristics
that were compatible with Christianity, especially making use
of its advanced code of laws and its collaborative view of the
roles and leadership of women. This legacy of the ancient

Druids forms a background, an "old testament," if you will, to the effort of the Celts to discover the true God. With reverence, then, for the total efforts of the Celts to reach out to the mysterious God-Presence to which every aspect of nature points, we will look together at the Celtic "new testament": the first thousand years of Celtic Christianity.

The material that follows divides the book into four parts. The first chapters fall under the metaphor of "healing wells," in which we discuss the characteristics of Celtic spirituality, its theological underpinnings, and its relationship to the life-views that preceded it. Part II, "Celtic Holy Women of Ireland," is self-explanatory. It narrates the legends and stories surrounding the primary Celtic holy women of the fifth through eighth centuries, in what is now Ireland. It reflects especially on their pertinence to our life and times. Part III shows us the "Pioneer Saints of Wales"; and Part IV introduces us to the early Celtic saints of Cornwall. Walk with us, then, in this holy pursuit, knowing that we do not travel alone, but in the presence of the One who draws us.

PART I

healing wells: springs of celtic spirituality

Cross of Muiredach, 10th Century, County Louth

CHAPTER 1

the
Celtic Soul

I n every culture there are elements deeply rooted in the
psyche of its people. These elements shape and propel
these people, flowing as they do from their natural bent
and unique giftedness, from their environment and its inter-
play in their lives, and their relationships with creation and
with divinity. So essential are these to the cultural heart of a
people that they may be called its "soul."

Emerging more than two thousand years ago, the Celtic
culture extended throughout parts of Europe as far as Greece
and Turkey. Described by historians as proud and courageous, the Celts had their own language, art, and mythology.

Their strength was their communal appreciation and adapt-
ability; their weakness was their lack of central organization. Thus, as they were attacked, the Celts easily moved
from one place to another place that was more protected by
its natural surroundings. Ultimately, the Celtic people found
themselves in the more isolated districts of Scotland, Wales,
Cornwall, the Isle of Mann, Brittany, and Ireland. Because

of this insularity, the soul-traits of the Celts are preserved and encountered even in the Ireland of today.

The Celtic soul is intuitive, leaping readily beyond the here and now. It is imaginative, playing gleefully with the symbolic and mythical. It is inclusive, caught up in family and community. It is wide open in its hospitality. It is God-centered in its day-to-day orientation toward life. It is given to storytelling and song, in the company of friends, over a pint in the local pub.

A Celtic spirit sees God's action as integral to moment-to-moment living. Every aspect of life is enabled by God and enlivened by God. It is the kind of God-awareness that inspired many Irish mothers (including Bridget's mother, Bridie) to begin each day with the phrase: "In the name of God." The awareness of being immersed in the holy in the midst of a circle of love like a cocoon or a womb which God has woven around you–this is core to the Celtic understanding of life.

The daily spiritual practice of the Christian Celts from the fifth century on focused on holy Scripture, particularly the psalms and the Gospel of John, and on a deep reverence for the presence of Christ in the Eucharist, accompanied by a keen awareness of the feeling of Christ-with-us in the present, enfolding moment. An encircling format is evident in many prayers requesting the enfolding protection of God and the saints. This encircling is further reflected in the circular winding of pilgrims to this day at Ireland's holy shrines. Visitors move as they pray, clockwise, that is, sun-wise, around the sacred ruins, high crosses, and holy wells, repeating Hail Mary's and Glory Be's.

Encircling is also present in the "halo" at the meeting of the vertical and horizontal planes in the Celtic high crosses.

One sees it in the windings of the pilgrim path outlined at the labyrinth near the Peace Pole at the Curragh (an expanse of land retained in common since the time of Saint Brigit) between Kildare and Newbridge.

Encircling is reflected in Saint Patrick's Prayer: "Christ be before me; Christ be behind me; Christ be beneath me; Christ be above me." It is found in the words of an Irish prayer for protection: "May the encircling protection of God surround you—the encircling power of Christ's love."

This encircling motif may have had its origin in a pre-Christian trio of female goddesses named Banbha, Fodla, and Eriu. Each in turn met the first Celtic invaders. Banbha stopped them saying: "You cannot enter this land!" But the wily Celts told her: "If you allow us to enter, we will name this land after you." They prevailed by appealing to her ego. Next the Celts encountered Fodla, who also commanded them to stop. Again they prevailed by bribing her with the promise to name the land after her. Finally, they were met by Eriu, goddess of sovereignty, who was more welcoming than the others, offering them a sacred cup of wine. So, delighted with her, they promised this third goddess that the land would be named after her. Thus, Ireland had the triple name of "Banbha-Fodla-Eriu," which was eventually shortened to "Erin." Hence, there was already a willingness to accept the concept of the Trinity, since the myths of Ireland featured a trio of founding goddesses. Another pre-Christian trinitarian symbol is that of the Maiden, the Mother, and the Crone (or Hag). The Crone depicts the wisdom of the Aged One who has traveled life's cycle. In Ireland, the authors visited the Hag of Beara rock formation near Coulagh Bay and the nearby early monastic site of Saint Caitigern (or Catherine). According to legend, Saint Catherine turned the Hag of Beara to stone because she did not adopt the new Christian faith.

In the Celtic soul, distances in time and space seem to disappear into an awareness of the Divine "ever present." This time warp produces what we might term "historical inaccuracies," since the Celtic soul sees a "thousand years as yesterday." It is this kind of perspective that can recount the legend that Saint Brigit was present at the birth of Christ serving as midwife to Mary. This perspective doesn't for a moment accept the legend as factual; it is simply that the factual is not pertinent to the sense of the kairos of God's everpresence.

The Celtic soul takes seriously the pronouncement of Jesus that those who "do it to one of the least ones, do it to me." A similar awareness is told in a legend of Brigit who gave away to the hungry a basket of apples given to her by a wealthy admirer. On being admonished for distributing a personal gift to the indigent, Brigit's reply was: "What is mine is theirs." This is the world vision behind true Celtic hospitality. It is this value system that empowers our compassionate outreach in today's ministry of peace and justice. It enlivens this century's awareness of humanity as a global village for whose welfare each one of us is accountable.

Part of this timeless, distance-less mentality is seen in the concept of "thin places." For the Celtic soul, there are moments and places where the veil between present reality and the next world are so "thin" as to be nearly transparent. These are holy places or holy moments. Holy wells, cemeteries, high crosses, ruins of buildings—these are thin places where one cannot help being drawn to awe-filled prayer in the presence of the holy. The Celtic soul sees with a vision that can only be called "faith-eyes." A loved one is never far removed, whether merely absent or "with God," since the Celtic life of faith lives more in God's ever-present time (kairos) than in our chronological time (chronos).

Celtic spirituality is imbued with the sense of the "family of God," the communion of saints, as a spiritual bond connecting the living and the dead. The Irish wake, the tradition of accompanying the dead person on the journey into heaven, reflects this view. When the grandfather of one of the authors, Patrick Beale, died, he was waked in his cottage where family and friends gathered for an all-night vigil of storytelling, music, song, tears, food, and laughter. The next day, a large procession of family and neighbors accompanied Pat to the church for the liturgy and to the cemetery for Christian burial. In the Irish tradition, there is a Mass celebrated for the deceased one month after death, and it is common for family and friends to pray for a deceased loved one, for he or she is, after all, only a prayer away from us.

In the theology behind Celtic spirituality, and contrary to Augustine's view of sin as a vitiating and evil disruption of original innocence, is the gentler insight that sees human beings as essentially God-centered, since the creating light of God dwells within all persons. The divine light had been covered over and stifled by the inroads of sinful choices, but not extinguished. We are, as John's Gospel says, "begotten by God's light which is the light of humankind."

The Celtic liturgical calendar is flavored with expressions from the Eastern church. There are links with Syrian and Egyptian monasticism and the spirituality of the Fathers and Mothers of the Desert in the art work of the Book of Kells and in the depiction of Saint Antony of the Desert in some of the High Crosses, as well as in the beehive-style structures that were the early monastic cells. The deserts of the East were mirrored in Ireland by the rocky isolation of the Burren or of the Skelligs, those craggy mountains that push up off the coast of Kerry, or by the isolated islands such as Iona and Lindesfarne. Eastern-style monastic asceticism had been popularized in the West by Saint John Cassian whose influence is evident in Scotland, Ireland, Wales, and Cornwall.

The Celtic soul calls us to contemplate earth's beauty and join in the dance of life in celebrating the magnificence all around us. The Celtic soul calls us to spend time outdoors where mountains stretch our minds, and lakes and rivers refresh our spirits. In fact, the connection between water and spiritual power is a characteristic of Celtic spirituality. Lakes, rivers, springs, and wells are prominent in Celtic myth and associated with certain goddesses. In ancient times, women even went to holy wells to give birth. In Christian times, the Virgin Mary and several women saints, including Brigit, Ita, Gobnait, Monenna, Dymphna, Non, Tegla, and Winefride, are associated with springs, and water from these places is used in rituals and prayers for healing.

Celtic holy wells continue to be healing sanctuaries and serve as reminders of the influence of pagan traditions on Christian practice. In our present-day evangelizing efforts, a growing awareness exists of the incorporation of indigenous rites, rituals, and customs into Christian practice where these can be adapted. We are realizing that those peoples to whom we are reaching out already have keenly developed spiritual insights regarding the power of the Divine in their lives, for the same Holy Spirit draws and inspires every human being. Fortunately, in evangelizing the Celtic people in the early centuries of Christianity, the missionaries adapted all that was compatible with Christianity. That is why holy wells and their accompanying rituals are still common in Celtic spiritual practice.

One of these holy sites, Ladywell, near Ballinkill in County Leix, is still a popular pilgrimage site. Every year from before anyone can remember, people from Leix County gather at Ladywell to drink from, and bathe in, its waters, making a pilgrimage there especially on August 15 when a Mass is offered to celebrate the Feast of the Assumption of the Blessed Virgin into Heaven. The Ballyroan Brass Band plays and stories of cures and answers to prayers are retold.

A Celtic heart is a pilgrim heart. Celtic saints often undertook a journey to what they termed their "place of resurrection"—usually a site far away—where they were to perform some good work, and die there, stepping into eternity in exile from their earthly roots and home. Such a pilgrimage to one's place of resurrection was usually a long journey. Every pilgrimage, whether short or long, is an enactment of our life's journey. It represents the yearning heart, longing for an encounter with God. It is more than a trip or tour, because the pilgrim is seeking ardently for a meeting with the Divine without knowing exactly what surprise is in store. The pilgrimage is actually a response to God's invitation to relinquish control, to step out and risk all, without knowing the full consequences.

In Celtic tradition, the pilgrimage was far more rigorous than anything we might undertake today. The pilgrim set out, often by sea, to a totally unknown destination, believing that God was leading. It was always away from the familiar—and the familiar was Ireland, so dear for its hearth and family ties. Ireland's landscape with its "forty shades of green," its brilliant rainbows, its starry nights and air-crisp freshness was dear to every pilgrim-voyager who left with an awareness that there would most likely be no return. Such were the journeys of Colmcille (Columba) and Brendan the

Navigator, and of the women: Ia to Cornwall, Melangell to Wales, Cannera, Dymphna and others who traveled to far countries. For that matter, the same is true of Gobnait, who traveled without settling anywhere until "she would see nine white deer grazing together." That sign would signal the site for the establishment of her monastery, and the place where she was to await her resurrection. The "loose grasp" of a faith-journey in which the Christian allows God to be the captain of the ship and the guide of the traveler's steps is a mark central to the inner listening of Celtic spirituality. Such drastic pilgrimages of those early saints were called "white martyrdom."

At the heart of the Celtic women saints is a deep-rooted trust that life is good in joy and in grief alike. Now is the time for saintly women to arise from their neglected past and reveal for today's men and women the still-pertinent message of their visionary lives and prophetic witness.

Saint Non's Holy Well, original 19th century woodcut

CHAPTER 2

Celtic holy Women

OUR SACRED GUIDES
AND COMPANIONS

In Celtic society, women in early Christian times were protected by the Brehon law, and, far more than their Roman and Greek sisters, they enjoyed equality with the men in their society. They could be leaders, lawyers, judges, poets, rulers, warriors, teachers, spiritual guides, and foreign missionaries. They had the right to marry, divorce, retain possession of property, and rely on protection against sexual abuse. Of course, as in all societies, the law was not always upheld, and stories of rape exist in many of the legends of the female saints—a sign of the in-creeping of a more male-dominant model which, over the centuries, diffused the original system of equality found in Celtic lands. Because of its isolation as an island on the "edge of civilization," the Celts of Ireland give anthropologists of today a kind of time-warp view back into a society where the sexes were on an equal footing.

As male dominance made its inroads from the European continent, seeping into the Celtic lifestyle and thought patterns, other inequalities also crept in. A woman's right to property usually ceased at her death; but males did not have any restriction on bequeathing property. This may account for the shorter life span of monasteries established by women, and the longer life of those, such as Clonmacnoise and Glendalough, established by men whose land rights rested in male ownership. There are exceptions, as in the case of Killeedy, Killeevy, Kildare, Whitby, and Ballyvourney, where the foundations of women were long-lived and may have been sustained because of the patronage of a local chieftain or of the saint's own family. Other sites, such as Clonbroney, Killnaboy, and Bantry have little to mark them after fifteen hundred years. Some sites in Wales are well-kept, including those commemorating Melangell, Winefride, and Non, as a result of the custodianship of the Church of Wales and the Roman Catholic Church. Other wells of Wales, such as the well of Saint Tegla in Llandegla, are in desperate condition.

The partnership and equality of women and men can also be seen in the double monastery system. Both Brigit of Kildare and Hilda of Whitby founded monasteries in which women and men lived. Some believe that Ita's foundation in Killeedy was a mixed community. These monastic settlements, referred to as *conhospitae*, or double houses, included women and men, some of whom lived a celibate life while others were married couples with children, but all living as a Christian community, having dedicated their lives to Christ. All, whether married or single, were referred to by a term that translates as "religious." The Christian Celts at that time did not consider celibacy as somehow higher or more dedicated than marriage, as was the case on the European continent. Both

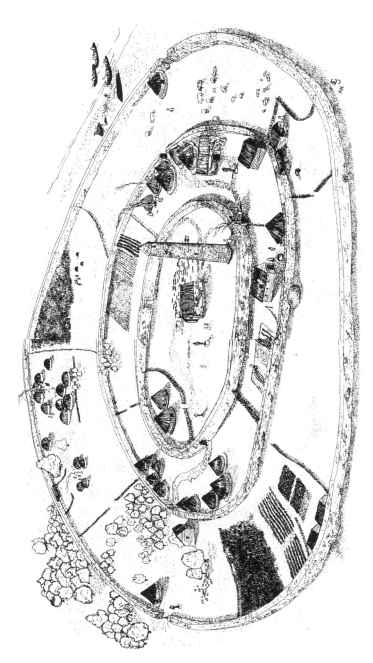

Reconstruction of a 10th century monastery

consecrated states were understood as holy and seen as complementary. The dualism that plagued the thinking of much of Western Christianity was not prevalent in Celtic lands until pressure from Rome following the mandate of 1139 made celibacy a requirement for all religious.

In double monasteries, men and women worked as equals. Scholars believe that women did the weaving of cloth and the sewing of ecclesiastical vestments, while men did the heavier work such as building, digging, and plowing. However, the overall authority within a double monastery often resided with an abbess who governed both the male and the female houses. Cogitosus, a seventh-century biographer of Brigit, says that Brigit and Conleth, whom Brigit selected to help her administer Kildare, "governed their church by a mutu-ally happy alliance."

These monastic settlements should not be confused in our thinking with what we envision as a monastery today with its elaborate structure, many wings, and attached buildings. A monastic foundation in the Celtic lands was a rath, or large circular mound of soil enclosing the living area, often topped by a fence of pointed sticks as a protection against wild animals. Within this defensive perimeter were cottages of wattle and clay or of stone (depending on what materials were available in the area) which were igloo-like in style. The monastery was inhabited by members of the local clan who had become Christian. Cragganowen, in County Clare, with its wattle huts and circular raths, provides a glimpse into Celtic life of ancient times. Kildare Cathedral houses a glass-encased model depicting a monastic settlement at the time of Saint Brigit.

Some scholars point out that women in the Celtic Church presided at various religious ceremonies. *The Life of Brigit* describes the investiture of Saint Brigit by Bishop Mel, nephew of Saint Patrick. He said: "Come, O holy Brigit, that a veil may be placed on your head before the other virgins." Then, Bishop Mel read from the words for the ordination of a bishop. While she was being invested, a brilliant fiery flame ascended from her head and Bishop Mel's assistant complained that a bishop's rank was bestowed on a woman. Bishop Mel answered: "But I do not have any power in this matter. That dignity has been given by God to Brigit, beyond every other woman."

Women's ministerial roles in the liturgy must also have been a feature of the church in Celtic Brittany. In the sixth century, three Roman bishops sent a letter to two Breton priests, Lovocat and Cathern, banning women from distributing the Eucharist: "You celebrate the divine sacrifice of the Mass with the assistance of women....While you distribute the Eucharist, they take the chalice and administer the blood of Christ to the people....Renounce these abuses...!"

The tradition of a Christian seeking a spiritual guide, mentor, soul friend or *anam chara* (in Gaelic) was a prevalent Celtic custom. Saint Brigit stated that a Christian without an *anam chara* was like a body without a head, so important was this spiritual friendship in living out the gospel. Women as well as men served as spiritual friends. This custom eventually influenced the entire Church and led to the institutionalizing of private confession for the sake of spiritual growth. There are stories of spiritual seekers coming to Saint Ita and Saint Samthann to reveal their sins and to receive guidance for their lives.

The center panel of this triptych found in St. Patrick's Cathedral in Armagh depicts Bishop Mel installing Brigit as abbess. Courtesy of the authors.

a Celtic Spiritual adventure

O ur search for the women saints of Ireland led us
on an adventure of discovery to the holy places
sacred to their memory. Devotion to many of these
saints is regionally based, except for Brigit, who is nation-
ally acclaimed in Ireland. Even in a particular locality, many
residents are unaware of the presence of a shrine to these
women saints, and it often takes more than one inquiry to
locate the spot down the twisting of some isolated country
road. Information about these hidden saints had to be gathered in bits and pieces. However, once we had arrived at a
shrine, there was clear evidence of an enduring reverence for
the holy place and its saint. Stone walls, wells, marked burial
mounds, and occasionally whole buildings were still identi-
fiable in spite of the passage of time. Pilgrims were still present
and praying, and caretakers were attempting to save the remains of these shrines. In Ballyvourney, for example, the
O'Herlihy family who were originally clan chieftains over-
see the care of Saint Gobnait's Church. It should be remembered that, like many other saints, these Celtic women were

canonized by popular acclaim, not by papal decree, show-ing once more the deeply rooted spirituality in the hearts of the people.

This timeless reverence was reiterated for us at Ballybuggy, County Laois, where one of the author's cousins, Joe Davy, led us to a back pasture to a place known as "Brigit's Rock." Here, says local tradition, Saint Brigit stopped to rest on one of her journeys, placing her hands on the rock where there can be seen two indentations the size of a human hand. There is a cleft in the rock, and pilgrims with any kind of head pain, earache, or similar malady still come to kneel and to place their hands in the "hand prints" of Brigit and their heads in the cleft of the rock, praying for Saint Brigit's inter-cession and God's healing.

The transcendent spirituality of the Irish is nowhere more evident than in this story of the trip to Brigit's Rock. As soon as we had learned of the rock in a neighboring pasture, we jumped into the car to seek out the little-known shrine. Joe called a local farmer on a cell phone to get permission to cross his field to the shrine. "You can cross, surely," the neigh-bor said, "but be careful to watch out for the ram." At the junction of two back roads, we arrived at a fenced field and padlocked gate. Here the car pulled to a stop. "What do we do now?" we asked. "We climb the fence," said Joe. The little band of pilgrims scaled the gate and set out across the pasture, all the while avoiding the ram, thistles, and nettles. Cell phones and automobiles appear to seamlessly merge with the ancient in Irish life today.

The ancient and the contemporary continue to intertwine as this following story illustrates. One dark, wet evening one of the authors was walking down a slippery slope to get to the foot of Saint Dymphna's well in Lavey, County Cavan.

She met an eighty-year-old man who had come to get a bottle of holy water for his sick wife. He did not see the path very clearly and he fell over an embankment. Providentially, he was not hurt. The spry old gentleman then picked himself up and stepped lightly across the stones in the river to the spot where, strangely, the holy well has an opening right in midstream. He balanced himself, reached over, dipped his bottle into the water flowing up out of the well, and then volunteered to get a bottle for the author. He stopped for a brief chat and then climbed the steps back to his car. Stirring experiences such as this one sum up the centuries-long life of Celtic piety. At these wells, people of faith find a life-giving water of divine love poured out anew because they have loved and believed much. Refreshed, they leave in the peace that God is still with us.

Come with us, then, on our holy pursuit of Celtic heroines, and expect your journey to be full of unexpected discoveries, little miracles, and constant surprises. Make with us a series of "pilgrim pauses" at each shrine where we will be drawn together into the circle of wisdom and strength radiating from each holy woman. May each circle be for us a thin place where we encounter the holy. May the prayers and reflections we draw from each saint's life nurture our spirits and, above all, may we allow this journey to transform us.

PART II

Celtic Holy Women of Ireland

Saint Brigit of Ireland, The Crosiers/Gene Plaisted

CHAPTER 4

Saint Brigit of Kildare

A REFLECTION OF GOD'S MERCY

The Spirit of Our God is upon me:
because the Most High has anointed me
to bring Good News to those who are poor.
God has sent me to proclaim liberty
*   to those held captive,*
recovery of sight to those who are blind,
and release to those in prison—
to proclaim the year of Our God's favor.

PARAPHRASE OF LUKE 4:18–19

Pilgrim Diary: Notes Along the Way

According to tradition, Saint Brigit built her monastery in Kildare beside a large oak tree around 480 A.D. In Gaelic, *Cill Dara* (Kildare) can be translated as "cell" or "church of

23

the oak." The cathedral in Kildare is built on the site of Saint Brigit's fifth-century foundation. Here are beautiful stained-glass windows depicting stories about the legendary abbess.

Still in existence are the foundations of the fire building where Brigit's sisters tended "Brigit's fire," a perpetual flame kept burning by Brigit and her nuns from the sixth century until the destruction of the monasteries in the sixteenth century. Fire is a symbol that reflects back to pre-Christian times but which is also associated with saints like Brigit and with divine power in Christianity. Some scholars believe that Brigit's foundation may have originally been a sanctuary of Druidic priestesses who converted to Christianity. (See M. Pollard, *In Search of Saint Brigid, Foundress of Kildare*, Armagh, 1987, cited in Rita Minehan, C.S.B., *Rekindling the Flame*, Solas Bhride Community, 14 Dara Park, Kildare, Ireland, 1999.)

Sister Mary Minehan, a Brigidine sister, and Sister Phil O'Shea came to live in Kildare in 1992. They opened Solas Bhride, a small Celtic spirituality center in the spirit of Brigit of Kildare. They welcome pilgrims from all over the world who come to Kildare to walk the ancient paths, pray at Brigit's wells, and connect with Ireland's legendary saint. The Brigidine Sisters, founded in 1807, are a restoration of the ancient order of Brigit. In 1992, they came to Kildare to re-connect with their roots and to reclaim Brigit in a new way for a new millennium. This led to the relighting of the flame of Brigit in 1993.

In both 1999 and 2000, we met with Sister Mary who shared traditional stories about Saint Brigit with us and guided us to the sacred wells of Kildare: Saint Brigid's Wayside Well, Saint Brigid's Well and prayer stones, Saint Brigid's Cathedral, and Saint Brigid's Parish Church. On one occasion we gathered with the Friends of Brigit around her flame in a prayer for healing. The spirit of Saint Brigit lives on in those who work for the full equality of peoples in the Church and in society, and who work to promote peace, reconciliation, justice, and conservation of God's good earth. (Note that the spelling of "Brigit" varies according to context and usage.)

Saint Brigid's Cathedral is owned by the Church of Ireland and was constructed in the twelfth century on the site of Brigit's abbey. In the churchyard is a timeworn round tower and a Celtic cross (without its top section) that may date as far back as the tenth century. Inside the cathedral are picturesque stained-glass windows depicting scenes from Brigit's life. Also worth noting is a *sheela-na-gig*, a primitive fertility stone figure hidden under the tomb by the door. In order to see it, you have to get down below on the floor.

Some scholars believe that *sheela-na-gigs*, such as the one in a medieval church in Killinaboy in County Clare, depict Saint Brigit with a wide-open womb even though she was a virgin. In Killinaboy, the sheela is carved on the top of the arch to the door. *Sheela-na-gigs* continue the representation of Celtic women as generous providers. These *sheelas* present a positive attitude toward female sexuality and honor birthing as a sacred experience. Like pre-Christian cultural icons, Brigit was associated with fertility and abundance. She was an activist who, mother-like, sought the health, well-being, and growth of her children. Perhaps today, *sheelas* can remind us that all creation is enveloped in the eternity of God's love.

Faughart, which according to folklore is the birthplace of Saint Brigit, is located near the border of south Louth and north of Armagh. Faughart is a peaceful place, surrounded by trees and a panorama of the Irish countryside, including the Gap of the North, the Plain of Muirthemhne, and the town of Dundalk. As you walk in through the entrance, you see a shrine with a statue of Saint Brigit on top of the roof. At the bottom of the steps leading to Brigit's shrine are various statues: Saint Patrick, patron saint of Ireland, Saint Columcille, the first missionary, Saint Malachy, twelfth-century reformer and archbishop of Armagh, Saint Oliver Plunkett who was martyred for the faith during the period when Catholicism was suppressed by Henry VIII. The statue of Brigit is located above all these, and looks as if she is suspended among the surrounding and majestic tall trees. To the left of the shrine is a holy well with its water spouting like a fountain.

Down the hill are prayer stones, stations of the cross, and a quiet stream. Several of the stones are identified as places where pilgrims come to pray for specific bodily ailments: there is the knee-marked stone, the waist-marked stone, the eye-marked stone, and so on.

A guidebook entitled *Saint Brigid of Ireland: Faughart Pilgrim's Manual* by John J. O'Riordan, C.Ss.R., provides a wealth of information on this shrine. It also gives both traditional and alternative versions of the stations for visitors. The stations are places where pilgrims stop to pray. "Doing the rounds," or moving from station to station, is an ancient prayer-style that Celtic people have practiced down through the centuries.

This resource also contains a description of one of the old customs associated with Saint Brigit that is being reclaimed today. This custom is known as the "Brideog and 'Gathering the Biddy.'" Children carry the Brideog, a cloth doll stuffed with straw from house to house, asking that the blessing of Brigit be upon each house. Or the parents would prepare a straw baby doll (made simply out of a baby's outfit stuffed with straw to resemble a body) in advance of the visit. On the eve of Saint Brigit's feast, January 31, when the family gathered for the main meal, one parent would carry the straw doll symbolizing Brigit out the back door (which represented the end of winter) and place the effigy at the front entrance, symbolizing the beginning of spring. The parent would knock and call out: "It is Brigit who knocks. Let Brigit in." Those inside the house would respond, "Brigit is welcome." The ritual was repeated twice more (three times in all) and then the parent would bring the straw doll representing Brigit through the door whereupon all would say: "Welcome to our table, Brigit. Let us make a toast. *Slàinte* (cheers)." The doll was then given the place of honor at the table.

The popular custom of the weaving of Saint Brigit's cross is believed to have started during a visit by Brigit to a dying pagan chieftain whom some sources identify as her father. To share her faith in Christ, Brigit wove a simple cross from the rushes strewn on the floor. From that time on, the woven rush cross has been identified with the saint.

The Brigit cross is usually made around February 1, Saint Brigit's feast day. After the cross is woven, it is blessed and placed above the entrance to a house, barn, or stable as a sign of protection and blessing for all who live within. (See the Appendix 5 for a description of how to make the Brigit cross and for prayers of blessing to accompany its installation.)

Another place where Saint Brigit is celebrated is in Saint Patrick's Roman Catholic Cathedral in Armagh which has some of the most exquisite stained-glass windows depicting scenes from her life. One window shows the clothing ceremony in which Brigit is presented with a white woolen dress. According to the story, each nun was asked to choose a beatitude which she would practice. Brigit chose "Blessed are the merciful, for they will receive mercy" (Mt 5:7). Being a reflection of God's mercy and love to the downtrodden became the cornerstone of Brigit's life, according to Elaine Gill in *The Book of Celtic Saints* (Blandford Press, 1996).

Encountering Saint Brigit

Brigit of Kildare was born around 450 A.D. at the time of transition from pagan to Christian Ireland. Legends say that Brigit was baptized and named by angels and that she was midwife to the Virgin Mary and godmother of Jesus. (Anachronisms did not disturb the Celtic mind!)

Saint Brigit was the daughter of a pagan Irish chieftain and a Christian slave woman. According to the story, Brigit's pagan father, Dubthach, was a prince, and her Christian mother, Brocessa, was a slave. Dubthach's first wife may have banished Brocessa to Faughart before Brigit was born. Custom says that Brigit may have been fostered to a pagan family who provided for her education and support. In her early years, she is likely to have worked on a farm, milked cows, and churned butter. Statues often depict Brigit with a cow at her feet. She was seen as the protector of farm animals and guardian of the harvest. When she reached the age of marriage, she rejected the suitors her father had chosen for her, dedicated her life to Christ, and became an abbess.

Brigit was the most prominent woman leader of the Celtic church. Her symbol was perpetual fire, representing wisdom, healing, poetry, metal-working, and the hearth. Although six lives of Brigit were written before the eighth century (and eighty during medieval times), it is difficult to separate fact from legend. Some theorize that she may have been a priestess in service to the Goddess Brid (patroness of fire and knowledge in the Druidic pantheon) before her conversion to Christianity was facilitated by her mother. Whatever the circumstances, Brigit and seven companions, robed in white, were baptized and formed Ireland's first religious community of women at Kildare, a name that means "church of the oak."

As Ireland's advocate of women's roles, she was a courageous risk-taker, healer, abbess of broad-reaching powers, founder of a school of metallurgy, successful administrator, and an energetic missionary. The force of her Celtic soul is a rich lodestone of the Celtic feminine which continues to challenge each new generation.

The stories and legends that follow are, in all likelihood, a blend of Christian beliefs and pagan elements, a mixture of the all-encompassing Druidic mother goddess with the dynamic post-pagan woman of compassion, generous hospitality, and charity to all. This blending was not condemned by Saint Patrick and later missionaries but was used as a way to interpret Druidic customs in Christian terms, so gradually the saints and feasts of the liturgical year supplanted the festivals of the gods and goddesses on the Druid calendar.

Brigit's previous authority as a high priestess may explain why Saint Mel, bishop of Ardagh, is said to have ordained her a bishop. The *Irish Life of Brigit* describes it this way: "When the hour of consecration had arrived, the veil was raised by angels from the hand of Mac Caille, the minister, and was placed on Saint Brigit's head. As she bent down during the prayers she held the ash beam which supported the altar, which was later changed into acacia, which is neither consumed by fire nor grows old during the passing of the centuries." Bishop Mel, Saint Patrick's nephew, who presided at the ceremony said: "Come, O holy Brigit, that a veil may be placed on your head before the other virgins."

Then, being filled with the grace of the Holy Spirit, Bishop Mel read the form of ordaining a bishop over Brigit. While she was being consecrated, a brilliant fiery flame ascended from her head. Mac Caille, Bishop Mel's assistant, complained that a bishop's rank was bestowed on a woman. Bishop Mel argued: "But I do not have any power in this matter. That dignity has been given by God to Brigit beyond every other woman. Only this virgin in the whole of Ireland will hold the episcopal ordination." Bishop Mel seems to say that only the abbesses of Kildare could be ordained bishop. Brigit's successors would continue to have high-level authority in the Irish Church. Indeed, other Irish bishops customarily sat at the feet of Brigid's successors until the Synod of Kells ended this custom in 1152. This monastic bishop was peculiar to Irish law, and indicated the powerful positions in the Irish Church of abbots and abbesses of the great monasteries. (This quote is from Oliver Davies (ed), *Celtic Spirituality*, New York: Paulist Press, 1999.)

Saint Brigit was an *anam chara*, or soul friend. This practice of spiritual companionship is a characteristic associated with Celtic saints. Brigit's own soul friend was the younger nun Darlughdach, who sometimes functioned as her ambassador. When Brigit told her that she expected to be dying soon, Darlughdach begged that they might die together. Brigit responded that Darlughdach would outlive her for one year, in order to succeed her as abbess. Brigid died on February 1, and Darlughdach died exactly one year later.

Another story is told about Brigit who, on one occasion, was dining with her foster son. She asked the young man if he had a soul friend. "I do," he answered. "Let us sing his requiem," replied Brigit, "for he has died. I saw when you had eaten half your portion of food that a portion was put in the trunk of your body, but that you were without any head. For your soul friend has died, and anyone without a soul friend is like a body without a head. Eat no more until you get a soul friend." Certainly this story can remind us of the great need for spiritual companions to accompany us on our journey to the Holy.

Brigit's early biographers describe her as a healer, curing lepers and giving speech to the dumb, turning water into ale, or stone into salt. A story is told that a nun of Brigit's convent became ill and desired milk, but there was no cow nearby at the time. Brigit filled a container with water, blessed it, changed it into milk, and gave it to the nun who recovered immediately.

On another occasion, a woman who was destitute came begging to Brigit. Brigit gave the woman her own garment and said that it would heal the disease of anyone to whom it was applied. It so happened that the woman was ill, but from that day forward suffered no longer from her illness.

In another case, a leper came to Brigit and asked for a cow. She said to him: "Which seems best to you, to take away a cow or to be healed of leprosy?" The leper said that he preferred to be healed of leprosy. Brigit prayed, and the leper was cured at once.

According to another story when Patrick and Brigit were on a missionary journey together, they did not have enough food to give to the crowd. Brigit inquired: "What food have you?" "There is none," replied one helper, "but one sheep and twelve loaves and a little milk." Brigit replied: "This is good, the preaching of God's word will be made unto us and we shall be satisfied thereby." At the end of the sermon, Brigit blessed the food and distributed it; as much food was left over as when they had started. In this case, Brigit and Patrick reflect a model of partnership in ministry and as well as compassion for the physical and spiritual needs of God's people. This is a model that can inspire us even today. This Brigit story is recounted by Ian Macdonald, in *Saint Bride* (Edinburgh: Floris Books, 1992).

Brigit was also a great friend of animals, as the following story illustrates. A peasant accidentally killed the king's favorite pet fox. Brigit prayed and a fox came out of the woods and jumped into her chariot. She gave the fox to the king in exchange for the peasant's life. On another day, Brigit saw some ducks swimming in the water, occasionally taking wing; and being moved with affection for them, she commanded them to come to her. A great flock of ducks flew over to her, showing no fear as if they were used to people. She touched and caressed them for a while, before allowing them to fly back into the sky. She then praised the Creator of all things, to whom all creatures are subject. These animal stories are taken from *The Life of Saint Brigit the Virgin by Cogitosus*, as it appears in Oliver Davies (ed), *Celtic Spirituality* (New York: Paulist Press, 1999).

Brigit was also renowned as a peacemaker, for in her time there were many disputes that threatened to erupt into armed conflict. As Mary Condren in *The Serpent and the Goddess: Women, Religion, and Power in Celtic Ireland* (San Francisco: HarperSan Francisco, 1989) says: "...she caused enough confusion that she fooled each side into thinking it had won, thereby ending the battle without bloodshed."

Generous hospitality, a traditional characteristic of Celtic people, was also a hallmark of Brigit's life. Brigit was a woman of abundance. All were welcome at her table of plenty. She saw to it that there was more than enough food, drink, and love to nourish all who came to her hearth and home. The story goes that during one Easter season Brigit noted that there was not enough ale for seventeen of her churches. She changed water into beer to make sure that her churches were well supplied for the season.

On one occasion, Saint Brigit was traveling and, as evening drew near, she sought hospitality in a local woman's house. On account of her poverty, this women did not have the means to make a meal for Brigit. She broke up the loom on which she had been weaving to use it for firewood; and placing her calf that she had killed on the wood, she willingly lit the fire. The two then ate dinner and passed the night in vigils. The woman rose early to find another calf of exactly the same form and a wooden loom similarly restored. Thus, her miracle performed, Saint Brigit bade farewell and cheerfully set out on her journey.

Brigit's biographer Cogitosus recalls that she was a woman of compassion. No person who was poor or without resources ever left her presence without sustenance. One time, Brigit even gave the elaborate, feast-day robes of Bishop Conleth to the poor. When the bishop needed his vestments for an upcoming feast day, Saint Brigit gave him another set of vestments similar in both weave and color to those she had given away. Miraculously, Brigit had received replacements from Christ just when they were needed.

Another story told of Brigit involves a basket of apples which were given to her but which she promptly gave to some poor beggars. When her benefactor complained, Brigit replied, "What is mine is theirs." Even in her early life, Brigit managed to give away valuable items belonging to her chieftain father. Brigit's strong sense of justice was evident throughout her life.

Brigit's attitude of openness and generous welcome provides a model for us, especially valuable for the many people today margarinalized or even anathematized by their traditional religion. She lived the spirit of Jesus who himself hung out with outcasts, who challenged the authorities of synagogue and Temple, and who dined with the lowly. Brigit's inclusivity reminds us that we all belong at the Banquet of Love, the heavenly feast. Here all of us find our home, the place where we are loved totally, tenderly, and passionately in the heart of God. A table blessing attributed to Brigit says it all: "I should welcome the poor to my feast, for they are God's children. I should welcome the sick to my feast, for they are God's joy. Let the poor sit with Jesus at the highest place, let the sick dance with the angels."

St. Brigit's Well, Kildare, Ireland

Celebrating Brigit's Gifts for Our Lives

Brigit's hospitality, leadership, healing presence, closeness to God, her spirited promotion of peace are all qualities still needed. Let us celebrate and value Brigit's gifts to us in the following prayer service.

Opening Prayer

O God of compassion and healing,
You gave Holy Brigit to us as a sign of your love.
You caress us with the warmth of the sun,
You encircle us in Love's embrace.
You are behind us and before us.
You are above us and beneath us.
I consecrate all that I am to you.

Sit still for a moment and quiet your soul. Breathe in deeply the tenderness of God. Breathe out compassion for all living things.

Scripture

"I was hungry and you gave me food, I was thirsty and you gave me something to drink, I was a stranger and you welcomed me, I was naked and you gave me clothing, I was sick and you took care of me, I was in prison and you visited me."

MATTHEW 25:35–36

Intercessions

V. That I may give as gift the gifts I have received, I pray.

R. May I, like Brigit, be a reflection of God's compassion in our world.

V. That I may care for our marvelous planet with its animals and plants, I pray.

R. May I, like Brigit, respect and nurture all earth's creatures.

V. That I may share my food, clothing, home, and time generously, I pray.

R. May I, like Brigit, serve those who are in need.

Closing Prayer

Saint Brigit, you were a woman of peace,
You brought harmony where there was conflict.
You brought light to the darkness.
You brought hope to the downcast.
May the mantle of your peace
*   cover those who are troubled and anxious,*
*   and may peace be firmly rooted*
*   in our hearts and in our world.*
Inspire us to act justly and to reverence
*   all God has made.*
Brigit you were a voice for the wounded.
Strengthen what is weak within us.
Calm us into a quiet inner listening that heals.
May we grow each day into greater wholeness
in mind, body, and spirit. Amen.

SOLAS BHRIDE, KILDARE, 1997

Saint Brigit's Blessing

May Brigit bless the house wherein you dwell.
Bless every fireside, every wall and door.
Bless every heart that beats beneath its roof.
Bless every hand that toils to bring it joy.
Bless every foot that walks it portals through.
May Brigit bless the house that shelters you.

Saint Brigit's Table Blessing

Brigit's table blessing reflects her spirituality of womb-compassion: "I should welcome the poor to my feast, for they are God's children. I should welcome the sick to my feast, for they are God's joy. Let the poor sit with Jesus at the highest place and the sick dance with the angels."

Questions for Reflection and Discussion

1. Brigit was a woman of compassion. What challenges do we face in a world where 20 percent of the world's population own and consume 80 percent of the world's resources?

2. Brigit was a woman of hospitality. Who are the strangers whom we need to welcome?

3. Brigit was a woman of the earth. How can we protect and care for creation?

4. Brigit was a peacemaker. How can we be reconcilers and peacemakers today?

5. Bridgit Mary tells this story: Two swans glided serenely on the surface of the Erkina River in Coolkerry, near Rathdowney in County Leix, as Bridget and her father, Jack, stood on a bridge, gazing into its waters and reflecting on the years that they lived here in the small gray cottage bordering the river, with Bridie, wife and mother, who died in 1998. For Bridget and Jack just standing there was a moment of contact with family roots—a "thin place" where Bridie's presence was tangible. Where are the "thin places" that you can identify in your own family story?

6. Brigit was a woman of abundance. Reportedly her cows produced a lake of milk each day and an abundant supply of butter. What kinds of abundance do we need in our own lives?

Note: Saint Brigit's name has several spellings: Brigit, Brigid, Bride, Bridget. In Wales she is Ffraid. We use Brigit to refer to the saint, but the local spelling to refer to her sites, for example, Saint Brigid's Cathedral.

Saint Ita of Killeedy

CHAPTER 5

Saint Íta
of Killeeдy

FOSTER MOTHER OF
THE SAINTS OF IRELAND

Like a stag, a doe, longing for streams of cool water,
my whole being longs for you, my God.
My soul aches with thirst for God,
for a God that lives!
When can I go and see God face to face?
PSALM 42:1–2 *(INCLUSIVE NEW TESTAMENT)*

Pilgrim Diary:
Notes Along the Way

Saint Ita's biographical data and stories about her two sisters, Saints Fiona and Nessa, are gleaned from a collection called *Saint Ita* by Ide NiRiain (Ita O'Ryan), published in 1964 by Clonmore and Reynolds, Ltd, Dublin. Ide NiRiain's research is based on the *Vitae Sanctae Itae* found in manuscript form in the Bodleian Library at Oxford University.

This *Vitae* dates from the eleventh or twelfth century, but is a reworking of a prior and more ancient text, which makes it one of very few saints' lives coming close to being a contemporary record. Other resources used by Ide NiRiain include the lives of pupils of Saint Ita: Saint Fachtna and Cummene, Saint Mochoemog, and Saint Brendan.

Often, our resources in research for this book came from unexpected people and events. This amazing little book by Ide NiRiain simply dropped into our hands when we were relating to Bridget's cousin, Aiden, our plans for sleuthing out these many Celtic holy women. Aiden, who is a history buff, said: "I have a book on Saint Ita you can have," and promptly produced the small, four-by-seven inch volume from his bookshelf. Ita is of sufficient importance that a number of contemporary researchers of Celtic Spirituality have retold snippets of her life; but none is as thorough as this small, out-of-print volume.

Our journey to find Saint Ita took us down country roads some forty miles south of Limerick to the area still known as "Killeedy" (Cell or Church of Ita). To the right side of a narrow lane lies an open field (Cluain Credail: Meadow of Faith) and the ruins of a castle. To the left is a walled cemetery and the stone remnants of Ita's foundation. A statue of the saint, crozier-in-hand, stands watch over the quiet graves of the more recently deceased, and resting in its niche are the tokens of gratitude left by pilgrims, simple gifts: a medal, a picture, a small plastic statue. A bubbling stream runs close by, and in the cemetery is a muddy, circular indentation which was once Ita's holy well. To the right side of the area is a modern plaque that marks her burial place. A graveyard caretaker pointed out the various sites to us, and quietly left. A car pulled up behind ours on the roadway, and a woman stopped to pray for a few minutes. We lingered for prayer and picture-taking, awed that after fifteen hundred years there was this much activity on a weekday afternoon in August. It was evident that this saint was in her day, and is to this day, some-one very special! Her feast day is locally celebrated on January 15—her "Day of Resurrection" (the Celtic term for the day of death) about 570 A.D.

Encountering Saint Ita

She has been called "the Brigid of the South," and "radiant sun of Münster's Women," "Patroness of the Ui Connaill" ("O'Connells," a clan who lived here beneath Slieve Lua-chra—the Mountains of Luachra), and "Foster Mother of the Saints of Ireland."

This fair-haired daughter of royal blood was born to Kennfoelad (Faelan), King of the Desies, and Necta, his queen, in county Waterford about 480 A.D. Queen Necta's *anam chara*, or "soul friend," was Fintan, an old priest, who lived near their *rath*, (the circular earthen fortification which en-closed the living area of the king's clan and all who lived within that community).

When he saw Necta's baby daughter, Deirdre, he asked: "Why give her a pagan name? Look at her eyes! You can see her thirst for God!" And so he called her "Ita" (thirst or desire), and from then on that is what everyone called her: "Ita," the "thirsting one."

When Ita was in her teens, Faelan, her father, arranged an appropriate marriage for her. Her mother, on the other hand, understood her daughter's longing to consecrate her life to Christ and supported her in her decision to try to persuade her father to allow this. Theirs was a Christian household in a land where paganism still lingered. Legend has it that an angel appeared to Faelan, prophesying to him that Ita would go "to another part of the country and there serve God, and become patron of the people who live there." At any rate, with her mother's help, and at a moment when her father, at least temporarily, relented, Ita left home with a trustworthy traveling guide to find that place in the West where she knew God was calling her to found her monastery. This she did at the relatively young age of eighteen.

The journey took her to what would later be County Limerick, to the place still called after her: "Killeedy" (*Cill-Ide* or "Church of Ita") in the west of Münster. This, it had been revealed to her, would be her "Place of Resurrection." Here she opened a monastery on land provided by the local chieftain, who welcomed her, happy to have a holy woman settle in his territory. When he offered her the whole valley for her foundation, she would accept only four acres. "That is sufficient for a follower of the poor Christ," she told him. "I need only enough for a monastery and garden!" Here she trained the pious women who flocked to join her and opened a school where she could educate young boys.

Her younger sister, Fiona, eventually joined her community, assisting Ita by her organizational ability. Her baby sister, Nessa, when she reached her teens, also expressed a desire to join the community in the vowed life of a religious; and she did come to live at Killeedy. Ita, however, who had a keen gift of discernment, advised Nessa that marriage was an equally fine pathway to serving the good God and living a full life. Ita told Nessa that she was certain her sister was called to marry.

A young architect and builder named Behan, who had aided Ita in the building of her chapel, was quite taken with Nessa;

and it was Ita's discernment that Nessa and Behan were ideally matched. She advised her sister to give up her ideas of joining the sisterhood and to accept Behan's proposal of marriage. Nessa followed Ita's advice; she married, and ultimately gave birth to a son who was called Mochoemog (*Mo choem og,* meaning: my fair youth). The child received his education from his Aunt Ita, lived a holy life, and is also acclaimed as a saint.

Best known among Ita's students is Brendan the Navigator. His name is said to be a derivative of the pet name given him by Ita: *Braon Find* meaning "Fair Raindrop," since she looked on him as a "raindrop" or "gift" from heaven. Legend has him returning to his teacher and foster mother during his adult life on several occasions for counsel and guidance. On her advice, he undertook some of his more successful journeys.

Two stories of Ita tell of occasions of bilocation, one when she longed to receive the Eucharist from one of her proteges; and another when, lost in mystical prayer, she found herself present at a eucharistic celebration, many miles from her own monastery. Ita could be very practical in advising others, but at times impractical in directing her own spiritual life. It is told of her that her fasting was so extreme that her guardian angel, Mithiden, appeared to her, saying to her: "Your fasts are excessive; your penances are exaggerated." Ita began to cry because it was out of her intense longing for God that she had undertaken her long fasting and prayer. But Mithiden assured her: "God loves you." Cutting a slice from a loaf he had brought, the angel spread it with honey, gave it to her, and watched her eat. He poured milk in a cup and watched her drink. Then the apparition told her: "I have been the guardian of your purity. I have guided your thoughts toward

God. I have prayed constantly on your behalf. Now I will not leave you, radiant woman, until I have led you into the house of the Great King whom you love so much."

At one point, a young novice named Ailbhe, who had come to Ita for training in the spiritual life, confided to Ita a secret anxiety that was robbing her of happiness in the life at Cluain Credail. "Why," she asked her abbess, "does God love you so much that through you God heals the sick, gives you knowledge of the future, and enables you to prevail so forcefully against evil spirits? In prayer, you are absorbed in the most Holy Trinity; and they say you have even spoken with an angel!"

Ita blessed the girl with the Celtic gesture of signing her forehead with a cross, and replied: "You have already answered your own question. As you said, I pray always to the three Divine Ones. Anyone who does this, holding constant conversation in her heart with the Holy Trinity, will always experience the closeness of God. It is only because of the merciful Triune God that I have these graces you mention. It is because of this union with God, who can do all things."

The novice felt a burden lifted from her heart. Ita had not boasted of her long prayer-vigils and fasting, but rather of the merciful love of the Blessed Trinity and of the blessedness of being immersed in a consciousness of God's presence.

In advising Saint Brendan, one of her students and foster children, she describes to him what most pleases Christ. "I think," she told him, "that three things that please God most are true faith with a pure heart, simplicity of life with religious spirit, and generosity with charity. These three points have come down to us as hallmarks of Saint Ita's spirituality.

At her sister Nessa's request, Ita is said to have offered intercessory prayer for the Ua Conaill (O'Connells) whose lands were being threatened by raids by the Corcu Oche. "Holy Trinity," she is cited as praying, "Father, Son, and Holy Spirit, come to the aid of my children, outnumbered and without hope. In Your name they welcomed me. Help them now, against the inroads of men of Münster." By that night, the enemy had scattered, but the army of the O'Connells knew that they had experienced a miracle of deliverance.

In Saint Ita's old age, after years of being foster mother and teacher of so many, she is said to have experienced, again, a visit from her angel Mithiden. "What reward would you like God to grant you," the angel asked her, "for all your years of prayer and service?" Ita responded: "Just tell God that I long for only one grace: to hold *Iosagan* (Little Jesus) in my arms. It was *Iosagan* I always saw in the beautiful foster children I nurtured." The legend goes on to say that Mithiden left her, and Ita saw, picked up and craddled in her arms the Little Jesus, singing to him this lullaby called Saint Ita's Hymn. It is probably the first original Celtic poem by a female author.

Iosagan (Little Jesus)

O Jesus child, you are nursed by me
Here in my little place;
More precious far than golden coin
Is the gift to behold your face.
I nurse you, Jesus, in my home.
I nurse no common babe;
But night by night, against my heart,
You, who the world did save,
Rest, Jesus Child!

Little Jesus boy, my lasting good,
Your gift is joy and gladness!
I rejoice that I asked you to come.
Not to hold you!–What great sadness,
Jesus, holy angel child,
You are first above all other.
You visit in my little cell
To be cradled as by a mother,
My Jesus, Child!

Though noble kings and princes come
To my poor Cluain Credail,
From them I shall no gift receive
That I could love so well
So sing, my fellow virgins, sing
To Him who gives us all.
For He who dwells in heaven above
Is here in my little stall
My Jesus, Child!

Celebrating Saint Ita's
Gifts for Our Lives

Ita's many gifts to us are appreciated in this prayer ritual:

Opening Prayer

O Blessed Three-in-One, fill me with an awareness
of your presence and beauty!
May my baptism into Your Life, O Three-in-One,
fill me with Your virtue!
May my baptism into Your Presence, O Three-in-One,
protect me from consenting to evil.

> *May I be plunged again, Holy Trinity,*
>   *into the cleansing waters of my Baptism.*
> *May your waters surround me and shield me.*
> *May your embracing love encompass me.*
> *O Blessed Three-in-One, fill me with Your graces.*
> *Through the sweet water of my Baptism renewed,*
>   *fill me with Your graces.*

Reread the verses from Psalm 42 which so well reflect Saint Ita's steadfast pursuit of God. Recall that her very name, "Ita," chosen as a kind of "love name" to replace her given name "Deirdre," means "one athirst," or "thirsting for God."

Scripture

> Like a stag, a doe,
>   longing for streams of cool water,
>   my whole being longs for you, my God!
> My soul aches with thirst for God,
>   for a God that lives!
> When can I go and see God face to face?

PSALM 42:1-2
(INCLUSIVE NEW TESTAMENT)

Reflect on the insight of Saint Ita: to recognize the graces she possesses as the action of God, in and through her union with the Holy Trinity. She made it her practice to hold the Blessed Three-in-One ever in her heart. With a peaceful heart, now, call on the Blessed Trinity to allow you to rest in the Sacred Presence. In quiet, enjoy God's presence. As you are drawn to speak to the Holy One Within You, use your own Trinitarian words of praise, and offer intercession in union with the heart of Christ:

Intercessions

V. God of all mothering, help all those who are called to nurture others with patience, and with the insight to know how best to nurture.

R. Holy One, come, fill our need.

V. God of all fostering, enable us to foster the gifts of those whose lives we touch.

R. Holy One, come fill our need.

V. God of all teaching, show us how to expose others to the knowledge and wisdom they need in order to lead rich lives.

R. Holy One, come fill our need.

V. God, source of all integration and wholeness, heal us and make us whole; and aid us to help others toward wholeness and integration.

R. Holy One, come fill our need.

V. God of all hearts, show us how to generously share the gifts you have given to us; may we dedicate ourselves to your service.

R. Holy One, come fill our need.

Add any other intercessions which come to your heart. Then offer this prayer or one of your own as your closing prayer.

Closing Prayer

O Blessed, Holy Three,
Save me;
Shield me,
Embrace me,
Encompass me,
And this house,
And all in it.
Today, tonight!
And every day, and every night!
Yes, always, every single day and night,
Come Holy Three, to dwell here!
Holy Three, to be with me.
Holy Three, to live in me,
That my life may reflect Thee.
That I may think Your thoughts!
That I may do Your deeds!
That I may love with Your love.
Let me be Your resting-place!
In Your Name I am signed.
In the Name of the Trinity, I am bathed.
By the Holy Three-in-One I am embraced.
In return I love You, Blest Three!
How can I help but love you who are All-Goodness
and Light,
All Love and Compassion!
God of Love, be my Love, now and forever.

If you wish, take a stanza of Saint Ita's lullaby to the Infant Jesus which has special meaning for you. Read it over; perhaps sing it.

Questions for Reflection and Discussion

1. Saint Ita experienced the presence of an angel guardian, guiding, directing and praying for her. Much is being written about angels today. What are your thoughts about angels?

2. Ita suffered from misplaced zeal in her determination to please God. For this, the angel reproved her; urging her to take proper care of herself. What does this say to you about your life?

3. Reread Ita's advice regarding what most pleases God: (1) true faith with a pure heart; (2) simplicity of life with religious spirit; and (3) generosity with charity. Reflect on or discuss these ideas and their implications for your life.

4. What is Ita's attitude about holiness, both in the vocation of marriage and in the vocation of dedicated celibacy? Why is this a balanced view?

Saint Ita's well, Killeedy, Ireland
Courtesy Diocese of Limerick

CHAPTER 6

Saint Monenna of Killeevy

INTERCESSOR FOR PEACE

*Peace I leave with you; my peace I give to you.
Do not let your hearts be troubled, and do not let
them be afraid.*

JOHN 14:27–28

Pilgrim Diary: Notes Along the Way

Dolores Whelan from Dundalk, County Louth, led us to Saint
Monenna's ruins and well at Killeevy in South Armagh. This
site has become a focus for those who undertake a spiritual
journey to pray for peace. We followed Dolores across the
North Louth border into South Armagh, which is part of
Northern Ireland. While we were driving through a quiet
countryside of green fields dotted with sheep grazing on the
lush grass, we were shocked when out of nowhere appeared
a dozen British soldiers in combat gear. We were not stopped,
but it was an unsettling experience. After arriving at the site,

the Church of the Mountain of Cuilenn, known today as
Killeevy, we surveyed the ruins and the cemetery, and then,
led by Dolores, we climbed about a mile up a steep hill to
find a breathtaking view of Slieve Gullion. When we reached
the summit, we saw two donkeys playing and rubbing their
heads together as if they were hugging.

Slieve Gullion, a mountain amid a circle of volcanic hills,
is the center of much of the myth and legend of Ireland. Here
the Irish hero Cuchullain single-handedly defended Ulster
against the armies of Queen Maeve. And, here, the legendary Fionn MacCool was bewitched by Cuchullain's daughter. Later, in an eighteenth-century literary Renaissance, the
district around Slieve Gullion was known as the "District of
Songs," and the voices of the bards and the echoes of sacred
stories still seem to bring calm, creativity, and healing to the
deep tensions within the land.

Here is Saint Monenna's Well, lovingly framed in white,
situated near the ruins of two early churches which share a
common wall. A large cross-inscribed stone leans against the
outer wall of one of the churches. Saint Monenna's grave is
thought to be here. Prayer rags hung on trees near her well
are evidence of grateful pilgrims. If you make this one-mile
climb to Saint Monenna's Well, be sure to bring a symbol to
hang on this tree of thanksgiving.

According to John J. O'Riordain, C.Ss.R., early Irish bards
say that Monenna was also known as Darerca. She founded
a convent on Faughart Hill, a community of eight virgins
and one widow. This convent, and her later foundations,
proved to be one of the most important Irish convents in the
early years of the sixth century.

Later, close to this same site, the Canons Regular built
Teampall Bride na Hāirde (Saint Brigid's on the Hill) and

maintained it until the sixteenth-century Reformation. The church was destroyed in penal days. Today, there is a Romanesque church standing on this site at Kilcurry. It has stunning stained-glass windows depicting scenes from Saint Brigit's life, including her investiture by Bishop Mel. One striking window features Brigit with a crosier as a symbol of religious authority. The day we visited, we met three young girls who serve Mass. They wore large Brigit crosses over their white albs and processed in the sanctuary from the main altar to a side altar that was graced by a large statue of Brigit.

Encountering Saint Monenna

Very little is known of Saint Monenna or Saint Darerca of Killeevy. Scholars believe that her primitive life may have been one of the oldest Irish *vitaes*, written in the early seventh century around the same time as Cogitosus's *Life of Brigid*. According to the martyrology of Oengus, Monenna is the grand-niece of Eochu, the ancestor of the royal clan of Dalriada. According to legend, she was baptized by Saint Patrick who commissioned her to teach women converts. In her first group of vowed women was a widow whose child Lugar was adopted by Monenna. This young man grew up to be bishop of Ruscaigh, Cooley, County Louth. Ancient accounts also say that Monenna was Saint Patrick's sister and the mother of Bishop Mel.

Saint Monenna visited Brigit's foundation at Kildare where she was known for her great charity and humility. Saint Brigit appointed Monenna portress to the hospital and, in that role, she healed many sick and possessed persons. She was also such a giver to the poor, and so many sought her bounty, that her sister nuns complained that she gave too much away.

She pointed out that the poor were suffering members of Christ's mystical body and that God would certainly reward the nuns for any loss of temporal goods.

After a stay with Brigit, Monenna lived at Bishop Ibar's monastery in Ard Conais, an unidentified site possibly near Wexford. The Annals of Ireland report that Saint Brigit gave Monenna a silver shrine as a gift. During her time there, Monenna trained her followers in the rules of good living and, during a summer drought, she offered prayers for relief. During these prayers a spring with an inexhaustible supply of water miraculously appeared.

Monenna then moved back north to Faughart, County Louth. From there, she founded a monastery at a deserted place near Slieve Gullion. After her death, Monenna is said to have appeared to one other nun to reprove the sisters for adapting a relaxed Rule. You can read more about Monenna in Peter Berresford Ellis's *Women in Celtic Society and Literature* (Grand Rapids, Michigan: William B. Eerdmans Publishing Company, 1995).

Celebrating Saint Monenna's Gifts to Our Lives

Noragh Jones, our guide in Wales, also led a group of women to Saint Monenna's Well to pray for peace in Northern Ireland. As they were praying a ritual to heal the wounds of religious division, a military helicopter buzzed overhead. For them, the interruption of the peace prayers by a military helicopter was a poignant moment. In the spirit of peace pilgrimage, here is a ritual to celebrate the spirit of Saint Monenna. The ritual begins with a prayer to say before climbing to Saint Monenna's Well. This prayer is appropriate for any pilgrimage you may make. If you cannot physically accomplish this pilgrimage, you may wish to do so in your imagination.

Opening Prayer

> *We call on Brigid and Monenna,*
> *and all the saints of Celtic lands,*
> *to be our companions on the way.*
> *We call on the good people*
> *who have lived and prayed in this place*
>   *to pray for us now*
> *that we may have the strength and heart*
>   *for this pilgrimage.*
> *We gather all our hearts and minds into our walking.*
> *We gather all our longing and seeking into our walking.*
> *We gather all our sorrow for sin into our walking.*
> *We gather all our thanksgiving and delight into our*
>   *walking.*
> *We gather all our sorrow and heartbreak into our*
>   *walking.*
> *Let our every step be a prayer of all that it in us—*
> *All that we know and all that is dark and obscure.*
>
> *Bless the path on which we go.*
> *Bless the earth under our feet.*
> *Bless the friends who walk by our side.*
> *Saint Monenna, walk with us on our sacred journey*
>   *to peace.*

ADAPTED FROM JOHN J. O'RIORDAIN, C.Ss.R.,
FAUGHART PILGRIM'S MANUAL, DUNDALK: GENE LAMBE, 2000

Prayer When Arriving at the Well

Wellspring of the Ages, we gather at Saint Monenna's Well to pray for reconciliation and peace for ourselves, our loved ones, for Northern Ireland, and for our planet. As we walk around the well in a circle, or "do the rounds" as the Celts call it, we ask that we become aware that this is a "thin place," a place where earth and heaven meet, where the saints on earth and the saints in heaven become aware that there is only a transparent veil between us. Amen.

Scripture

> "By the tender mercy of our God,
>   the dawn from on high will
>   break upon us,
> to give light to those who sit in
>   darkness and in the
>   shadow of death,
>   to guide our feet into the way
>   of peace."

LUKE 1:78–79

Tree near Saint Monenna's Well, Killeevy, Ireland.
Courtesy of the authors.

Meditation and Reflection

We invite all armchair pilgrims who cannot be with us at Saint Monenna's site, as well as those who can be there in person, to join us in spirit and prayer for the following meditation.

Begin this meditation by playing soft instrumental music.
Take time to be still. You have just completed your climb up
the mountain to Saint Monenna's site (either in your imagination or in fact). Enjoy the panoramic view of the landscape of Slieve Gullion. Notice the green fields covering the
land like a patchwork quilt. It is quiet. Be attentive to the
rhythm of the earth. Marvel at things great and small that
move around you. Listen to the birds sing. Watch the sheep,
donkeys, and cows graze in the fields. Feel the wind caress you.

Breathe the fresh air slowly in through your nose and out
through your mouth for several minutes until you feel relaxed and calm. Watch the clouds leap across the sky in an
ever-changing pattern. Dance with God through your fears
and tears and into the Heart of Love.

Recall that Jesus told the Samaritan woman: "I am the
Living Water." Use a water metaphor as a mantra or prayer
phrase to express your longing for reconciliation and peace in
your life. Use one of the following or create one of your own.

- *Healing Waters, wash away my guilt.*
- *Creator of Earth, reconcile our global community.*
- *Sacred Spring, heal the hurt within me/us, within my relationships, within our world.*
- *River of Peace, rescue our polluted world.*
- *Well of Compassion, fill us with your justice and peace.*
- *Ocean of Goodness, may we reflect your care and wisdom.*

As you walk around the well, use your prayer phrase as
you feel the earth with your feet. As you walk, become aware
that the Healing Presence is with you now and on your life

journey. Become conscious of any burden that you carry for self, for others, for all of earth's creatures.

Then, when you feel ready, come to Saint Monenna's Well with your need for reconciliation, peace, renewal for yourself and/or for others. The Spirit of Love is with you, waiting to embrace you and all whom you carry in your heart. The Holy One makes sacred all things. Every mistake or failure in life can be "blessed."

Cup your hands and fill them with cool water. Bless, drink, or wash in this life-giving spring. Let it fill you, heal you, refresh you, and transform you. When you are ready, go over to the tree beside the well and hang on it a symbol of a blessing you have received today.

Closing Prayer

Saint Monenna, and our heavenly friends, we thank you for being with us this day. We take the peace we have celebrated here with us to home and hearth. As we descend this hill, we pray this traditional Gaelic pilgrimage prayer:

> *May God shield us by each sheep drop.*
> *May Christ keep us on each rock-path,*
> *May the Spirit fill us on each bare slope,*
> *as we cross hill and plain,*
> *Who live and reign*
> *One God forever and ever. Amen.*

ADAPTED FROM BRENDAN O'MALLEY,
CELTIC BLESSINGS AND PRAYERS

You may wish to conclude this prayer service with the Circle Dance (see Appendix 4) in honor of the blessings of the Spirit.

Questions for Discussion and Reflection

1. Little is known of Saint Monenna's life. Yet her well is still a place of pilgrimage and prayer. Why is it important to reclaim women like Monenna and share their stories today and with future generations? What benefits can accrue?

2. An old tradition has it that Saint Monenna never ate a sufficient amount of food to alleviate hunger pangs, and that she wore coarse garments in the manner of Saint John the Baptist. What does it mean to live a holy life as a ordinary Christian today?

3. Saint Monenna lived at a time of great conflict. How can we bring reconciliation and peace in conflict situations in our time?

4. How can we bless and transform our failures or messes into blessings? Which of our failures is most in need of transformation?

5. In addition to a "prayer rag" of thanksgiving left on a tree near Saint Monenna's Well, other offerings are also left: a stone to add to the cairns there or a gift of flowers and fruit. What emblem of gratefulness would you leave? For what are you grateful at this point in your life?

Lush green pastures on the shores on Bantry Bay, in County Cork. Corbis Images

CHAPTER 7

Saint Cannera of Bantry Bay

PATRON OF CELTIC PERSISTENCE

In the presence of God and of Christ Jesus, who is to judge the living and the dead, and in view of his appearing and his kingdom, I solemnly urge you: proclaim the message; be persistent whether the time is favorable or unfavorable.

2 TIMOTHY 4:2

Pilgrim Diary: Notes Along the Way

The town of Bantry in County Cork is nestled beside Bantry Bay, one of the finest harbors in Europe. On the edge of the Atlantic Ocean, Bantry Bay welcomed fleets from England, Spain, and France, whose captains paid harbor fees to the O'Sullivan clan who controlled the bay in ancient times.

The town of Bantry lies in the center of an age-old region that still bears remnants of megalithic and neolithic monuments (wedge tombs, stone circles, boulder burials and the Ogham Stone which is reputed to be the tallest in the world) that pre-date the Pyramids and ancient Greece. Here among palm trees and semi-tropical flowers was born Saint Cannera, a holy virgin and hermitess. At first, we found no evidence of any remains of Saint Cannera's hermitage in the Bantry Bay region. However, we were lucky enough to find out about this spirited woman at a local bookstore. The owner had written a book about the history of Bantry and gave directions to the shore of a contemporary campgrounds where her hermitage is believed to have been located. The rhythm of the lapping waves on the rocks provided a scenic backdrop for picture-taking of yet another soul-filled Celtic spot where God has touched the earth.

Encountering Saint Cannera

Cannera lived in a small hermitage near Bantry Bay. Scholars think she may have founded three monasteries. One night during prayer, she had a powerful vision of fire flaming above all the churches in Ireland. The brightest flames rose from the monk Senan's dwelling on Scattery Island. With only the light from the fire to lead her, says the legend, Cannera walked upon the sea until she arrived on the island—a distance of more than two miles from shore. Senan welcomed her and advised her to make her home with a nun living on a neighboring island.

"This is not why I came," Cannera replied, "But that I may find hospitality with you on this island."

Senan protested: "Women cannot enter on this island."

"How can you say that?" inquired Cannera. "Christ came to redeem women no less than to redeem men. He suffered for the sake of women as much as for the sake of men. Women as well as men can enter the heavenly kingdom. Why, then, should you not allow women to live on this island?"

"You are persistent," admitted Senan. So Senan changed his mind and allowed her to stay. After Cannera had received the Eucharist from him, she died immediately. At high water mark, Senan's fellow monks dug a trench on the edge of the shore and buried Saint Cannera. Her grave is identified by a flag off the island and is partially covered by the sea. Safely in heaven, Cannera could cause no more problems for Senan.

Cannera died around 530 A.D. According to custom, sailors invoke Cannera's intercession before embarking on sea voyages. Until just recently, seamen believed that pebbles from Scattery Island protected the holder from shipwreck. January 28 is celebrated as Saint Cannera's feast day.

In order to understand the freshness of Cannera's assertion of mutuality and equality in Christ, it is helpful to have an understanding of the role of women in the first centuries of Christianity. Elisabeth Schussler Fiorenza's *In Memory of Her* (New York: Crossroad, 1986) asserts that women held equal leadership roles and responsibilities in the early Church. The Gospel of Mark, for example, paints a positive picture of female disciples and praises women as true believers. "The unnamed woman who names Jesus with a prophetic sign-action in Mark's Gospel," observes Schussler Fiorenza, "is the paradigm for the true disciple....This is a politically dangerous story. While Peter has confessed, without truly understanding it, 'you are the anointed one,' the woman anointing Jesus recognized clearly that Jesus' messiahship means suffering and death." Jesus affirms the woman's prophetic gesture for all time by saying, "Truly I tell you, wherever the good news is proclaimed in the whole world, what she has done will be told in remembrance of her" (Mk 14:9).

The Christian community was portrayed in the Gospel of John as a community of friends and equals in which women like Mary of Magdala, Martha, and Mary of Bethany played prominent roles. It is clear, for example, from the Gospel of John and the Gospel of Luke that both writers experience a community in which women ministered as eucharistic leaders, preachers, and deacons. In Luke's church, well-to-do Hellenistic women even hosted the eucharistic celebrations in their homes. Luke describes Jesus' reproof of Martha and his affirmation of Mary.

Rose Sallberg Kam (in *Their Stories, Our Stories*, New York: Continuum, 1995) believes that this negative reaction to Martha did not reflect the attitude of Jesus to women whom he treated as disciples and equals. Kam points out, by way of explanation, that the Gospel of John was written around 100 A.D. when the official roles of women were becoming more limited. Yet, the Gospel of John also "places on Martha's lips a profession of faith in Jesus as Messiah that Mark 8:29 assigns to Peter. For the Johannine community, Martha is thus identified as holding no less than apostolic authority."

It is no wonder, then, that for several centuries, debates continued to rage over the role of women at the Eucharist and in the Church. This debate leads us back to Cannera who asserted the egalitarian attitude reflected by Jesus and the early Christian communities.

Those who believe in the equality and partnership of women and men as demonstrated from the earliest days of Christianity would relate well to Cannera's story. This spunky, courageous Irish lady would be a great model for twenty-first century workers for equality and justice in Church and society. She presents a paradigm of a strong and loving confrontation with male authority that goes to the heart of the matter: Are women created in the image of God or not? Did Christ die for women? In Christ, are women and men equal or not? Are women indeed *imago dei?*

Cannera spoke her truth directly to Senan. She had responded to God's call. She presented herself as an equal and partner, and this is how she expected to be treated. We will never know if Cannera and Senan would have founded a double monastery and worked harmoniously together for the Gospel as did some of the other Celtic saints. It is probably safe to assume that Scattery Island would never have been the same if the independent-minded Cannera lived there. Certainly, Elizabeth Johnson's description of the feminist agenda applies to the fifth century as much as it does to the twenty-first century: "Christian feminist thinking seeks a new wholeness, a new community of the mutuality of equals.... Mutuality is a form of relation marked by equivalence between persons. It involves a concomitant valuing of each other, a give-and-take according to each one's strengths and weaknesses, and a common regard marked by trust, affection, and respect for difference all this in contrast to competition, domination or assertions of superiority" (quoted in "Jesus and Feminism," Maureen McCormack, *Courage Newsletter*, Loretta Women's Network, Fall 2000).

Celebrating Saint Cannera's Gifts to Our Lives

Cannera is a soul friend and source of encouragement and empowerment. We hope that the glory of God's Presence that led Cannera will be a radiant light illuminating our steps in the journey toward full equality. More than ever, we need dedicated advocates like our fifth-century sister, Cannera. In the following ritual, we celebrate Saint Cannera's saintly persistence.

Opening Prayer

Saint Cannera, may we be courageous trailblazers like you, unafraid to afflict the comfortable, name the sin of bias, and live the vision of radical equality at the heart of the Jesus-vision in the Gospels.

May we be advocates for all women and do all that we can to advance the cause of their equal status. With you, we dream a new vision of mutuality and partnership as we pray in the name of Jesus Christ. Amen.

Scripture

"At about three in the morning, Jesus came walking toward them on the lake. When the disciples saw Jesus walking on the water, they were terrified. 'It is a ghost!' they said, and in their fear, they began to cry out.

"Jesus hastened to reassure them: 'Don't worry, it's me! Don't be afraid!'

"Peter spoke up and said, 'If it is really you, tell me to come across the water.'

"'Come!' Jesus said.

"So Peter got out of the boat and began to walk on the water toward Jesus. But when he saw how strong the wind was, he became frightened. He began to sink, and cried out, 'Save me!'

"Jesus immediately stretched out his hand and caught Peter. 'You have so little faith!' Jesus said to him. 'Why did you doubt?'

"Once they had climbed into the boat, the wind died down.

Those who were in the boat showed great reverence, declaring to Jesus, 'You are indeed God's Own!' "

MATTHEW 14:25–33 (*INCLUSIVE NEW TESTAMENT*)

A Prayer Celebrating Courageous Women

V. Cannera, as one gutsy Irish woman, you believed that women were also friends of Jesus, and you gave voice to your vision.

R. May all who see us, see Jesus Christ.

V. Cannera, accompanied by the fire of the Holy Spirit, you knew God was with you. You experienced God's glory in your vision. You insisted to Senan that you came to live in mutuality.

R. May we see the glory of God in each person.

V. Cannera, you knew that your experience revealed God. You did not return to your hermitage and pout when Senan rejected you. Rather, you hung in there and persistently made your case.

R. May we speak the truth with love.

V. Cannera, show us the way to Passionate Love. May we act as if our vision of the future is now a reality.

R. May we experience the joy of the Risen One in our waking and sleeping, in our dreams and desires.

Now be silent and still. Be aware of God's dream for you. Let the heart of God speak to your soul. Is it time for you to "walk on water"? Are you called to be a "courageous" person in quest of some good?

Scripture

"But Jesus said, 'Let her alone. Why do you criticize her? She has done me a kindness. You will always have poor people among you, and you can do them good whenever you want, but you will not always have me. She has done what she could. She has anointed my body and is preparing it for burial. The truth is, wherever the Good News is proclaimed throughout the world, what she has done will be told in her memory.'"

MARK 14:6–9 (INCLUSIVE NEW TESTAMENT)

In Memory of Mentors

On a piece of paper, make a list of women who have been a special blessing in your life, women who have inspired you, women who have challenged injustice, women whom you wish to remember. You may wish to take a few minutes and write a special message to one of the women on your list, expressing your feelings of appreciation and offering a prayer of thanksgiving for them.

In Memory of Holy Women

From your list, chose one woman whose story you want to remember. If you are in a group, pass a candle around. The person who has the candle shares why she/he chose a certain woman. If the group knows beforehand that they will be sharing these stories, each person could bring pictures, symbols, mementoes to share with the group and place in a memory book. After sharing, the person then places the candle on the table. As each person puts a candle on the table, the group says together: "We will remember you. We will give thanks for your gifts to us."

Intercessions

V. For ordinary women who open their hearts to others, we pray.

R. We behold the image of your creation, O God.

V. For women who work hard to nourish and nurture others, we pray.

R. We behold the image of your creation, O God.

V. For women who live as true partners and equals with men in Church and society, we pray.

R. We behold the image of your creation, O God.

V. For those like Cannera whom history forgot, and those like Senan whose virtue was remembered, we pray.

R. We behold the image of your creation, O God.

V. For those who are restructuring our world and our Church into a more just and inclusive family, we pray.

R. We behold the image of your creation, O God.

V. For women leaders especially *(name women for whom you want to pray)*, we pray.

R. We behold the image of your creation, O God.

V. For women who minister in all walks of life, especially *(name women for whom you want to pray)*, we pray.

R. We behold the image of your creation, O God.

Closing Prayer

Saint Cannera, we remember you. You didn't take "no" for an answer. You knew that women were equal and that in Christ all are one. May we be strong and persistent in our work to lift the second-class status of

*women around the globe. Let us take courage and, like
you, let us "walk on water" into the radiant heart of
God. Amen.*

Questions for Reflection and Discussion

1. Saint Paul says, "In Christ there is no Jew or Greek, slave
   or citizen, male or female. All are one in Christ Jesus (Gal
   3:28, *Inclusive New Testament*). How can this promise be
   extended to the present day?
2. Saint Cannera's persistence and faithfulness to the Gospel
   is a good example to everyone. How do we show our own
   persistence and faithfulness to the Good News?
3. Sailors who visited Scattery Island often took pebbles and
   drilled holes in them to make a necklace. This necklace
   was presumed to save the wearer from shipwreck. What
   kinds of protection would be most useful to you at this
   point in time?
4. Create a "pattern prayer" to celebrate women as equals
   and partners in the gospel.

CHAPTER 8

Saint Gobnait of Ballyvourney

GOD-SEEKER AND PURSUER OF JUSTICE

The wisdom of the humble lifts
their heads high,
and seats them among the great.
Do not praise individuals for their
good looks,
or loathe anyone because of
appearance alone.
The bee is small among flying creatures,
but what it produces is the best
of sweet things.

SIRACH 11:1–3

Pilgrim Diary: Notes Along the Way

Saint Gobnait came to our attention quite by accident, or should we say by Divine Providence, at a retreat center in Cork when fellow retreatants heard of our plan to travel to a nearby beauty spot, Gougane Barre, County Cork, where mountains and a lake meet in a luxuriant valley. "If you're going there," they said, "you should go to Ballyvourney to Gobnait's shrine." Gobnait is a saint greatly revered in the immediate vicinity of Ballyvourney, but not well-known or chronicled beyond her part of County Cork, near Macroon.

Our journey took us over circuitous country roads until, with some pointing by local residents and a few false turns, we saw signs for a holy well off to the right, and guideposts indicating that a little farther on would be a cemetery, chapel, shrine, and additional holy well sacred to this local saint.

At the top of a hill and to the left was a modern cemetery guarded by a large white statue of Gobnait and a marker indicating what had been "Gobnait's house." Praying the rosary there, we met a local woman named "Gobnait Abina" who comes daily to pray at her patron's shrine. Across the road, on the right, lies a more ancient cemetery where the grave of this seventh-century saint is clearly marked. Here, also, are the walls of her chapel, still intact. The "shrine-keeper," Donald O'Herlihy, who faithfully oversees the care of the property, filled us in on details we might otherwise have missed. The O'Herlihy family, we learned, as leaders of the clan, were entrusted with this duty from earliest times; and have continued it, faithfully, to this day.

Built originally in Gobnait's time, local citizens in the twelfth century restored the chapel to its present state, replacing toppled stones. It is quite sturdy, with arched window and door openings, but without a roof. The wooden roof, Mr. O'Herlihy explained, had been removed in the sixteen-hundreds by local residents to protect the structure from burning by Cromwell's raiders and to save the edifice from being used as a stable for horses. The timbers they hid behind a large rock in a nearby field; and, although the lumber has long since rotted, the rock is still spoken of fondly as "the rock of the wood."

A little pamphlet called "Saint Gobnait of Ballyvourney" by Eilis Ui Dhailigh (Ellis O'Daley) is available in a local convenience store in the present-day town of Ballyvourney for a little over one euro. It narrates several stories about Gobnait, and includes a map of her shrine area with instructions for "making the rounds"—an ancient pious practice undertaken by pilgrims even to this present day.

Encountering Saint Gobnait

Little is written of the holy woman Gobnait in most of the sources that refer to Celtic saints. In her own Ballyvourney, County Cork, however, Gobnait is still quite prominent. Many women of the area bear her name or that of her sister Abina, or both together. A long-held oral tradition says that her sister, Abina, joined Gobnait's community as one of her nuns. However, the name Abina may just be a version of Gobnait's name since "Abby," "Abigail," and "Deborah" are cited as English versions of her name. Deborah is the equivalent of Gobnait in Gaelic and means honey bee.

Gobnait was not a native of Ballyvourney. She came there from "far away," so the story goes. One tradition claims that her father was a pirate and that she docked at Fionntraigh, where an angel appeared to her telling her not to return to the ship, but rather to journey to a place where she would see nine white deer grazing. At that spot she was to establish a monastic settlement.

The Martyrology of Donegal speaks of her as "the virgin in the big bogland in the south of Ireland" where one can find her "ceall" (church or cell).

Inhabitants of Inisheer in the Aran Islands tell a different story. They claim that Gobnait spent time on their island, and that she had come from the Cliffs of Moher across the sea to escape some unnamed but dangerous threat to her well-being. They maintain that it was at their church, *Cill Gradh an Dombain*, that she was visited by the angel. From here, they say, she left for the mainland, traveling clockwise, southward, to Ballyagran, where there is a holy well in the graveyard in Kilshannig, honoring a "Saint Abby"—an English form of the word "Gobnait." Some believe that Saint Abby, also known as Abigail, and Saint Gobnait were the same person. Others maintain that Abby and Gobnait were two different people.

From there, Gobnait crossed Blackwater and traversed the Boggeragh Mountains, stopping near Macroon, where she saw three white deer. But this was not the prophesied number she was looking for; so, she continued on to Killeen. There she saw six deer; but, again, this did not fulfill the angel's words. She went further southward. Across the Sullane River and up a wooded hill she saw them—nine white deer grazing. This was the spot called *Gort na Tiobratan*. Here she built for herself a simple cell and prayed in gratitude to God who had led her to her "place of resurrection."

Young girls came to her, seeking to take the white veil as members of her community. Around her circular stone house they built clusters of wattle huts with enclosures of stone as cells for the members of the little community.

They herded sheep and cows, made butter and bread, and kept a hive of bees. (Gobnait was reputed to be a masterful beekeeper.) It was a self-supporting settlement, including a limited amount of metal and bronze workmanship among its craft output. Vegetables and wild berries added to their daily fare, and their main meal they shared each evening.

This little community was an integral part of the larger, surrounding community, giving their neighbors special care, and particularly ministering to those who were sick or in need.

In true Celtic tradition, Gobnait sought guidance from an *anam chara*, Saint Abban, whose church was a quarter of a mile from her settlement.

Several miracles are attributed to Gobnait, and these were performed in service to the people of Ballyvourney. A band of cattle thieves attempted to steal the cattle of the neighborhood; but Gobnait let loose a swarm of bees, and the robbers abandoned their rustling in terror.

Another time an enemy began to build a defense on a high rock, intending to control the vicinity and its people by his armed power. The legend says that Gobnait hurled her heavy, agate bowl at the edifice, boomerang-like, and reduced it to rubble. Again and again she repeated her attack every time the enemy attempted to rebuild; until, finally, he abandoned his effort in dismay and left the territory. This bowl, or bulla, is kept sealed in a cavity in the south corner of the west gable of her church and is one of the places where pilgrims stop to pray during their "making of the rounds." On another occasion, Gobnait is credited with stopping the plague through her prayer and fasting.

Caretaker Donald O'Herlihy pointed out two significant carvings in the stone of Gobnait's church that we might, otherwise, have missed. One was a *sheela-na-gig*, a fertility symbol, which seems to have survived its pagan inception to convey, as a Christian symbol, the church as the womb which enfolds us. This is carved into the stone at the arch of one of the church's windows. The second is a face carved in a stone in the facade above the chancel.

It is said to be the face of one of the stone masons employed to build the church. One night he stole a horse and a set of mason's tools, and set off at a gallop to escape with his booty. On and on he galloped at a furious pace, to put as much distance as possible between himself and Ballyvourney before dawn. But, much to his consternation, as the sun rose, he found he was still outside Gobnait's church. He had been circling it at a gallop all night long. The penalty for his offense was that his image was cut in stone and enshrined above the chancel arch of the church.

No one knows, for sure, how long Gobnait's monastery endured. It may have continued to function well into the twelfth century or beyond. The fact that the O'Herlihy family were, and still are, its caretakers suggests that it had a long life in the community of Ballyvourney.

Even when the O'Herlihy's lands were confiscated and given over to a Protestant overlord and when the land where the shrine is located became non-Catholic property, devotion to this holy place continued. There is no record of the shrine's date of closure, but it would have ultimately suffered extinction either under the suppression act of Henry VIII or with the anti-Catholic activity of the Puritan Era. Amazingly, for the four to five hundred years that have passed since those historical events, the people of Ballyvourney have saved, supported, and held sacred their shrine and the memory of Gobnait, a seventh-century heroine and holy woman.

An oaken statue of Gobnait from the thirteenth century was given to the local church by the O'Herlihy family in 1843 and is still exposed for veneration on festive celebrations in her honor. Gobnait's intercession is especially sought for by parents of mentally and physically disabled children.

Gobnait's feast day is celebrated on February 11, which, fittingly, is also World Day of the Sick as well as close to Saint Brigit's feast day on February 1. Saint Gobnait's Day marks the start of spring, the time for planting, and was celebrated with much festivity as a local holiday. A general pilgrimage is also held nearer to Easter when the weather allows greater numbers to participate. The prayer for the day reads in translation: "O Gobnait, bring us safely through the coming year, and save us from every harm and infirmity, and from smallpox."

A pilgrim to the shrine customarily visits several sites on the premises:

- Gobnait's "house"—an area designated near her statue
- Gobnait's grave
- The church
- The church interior
- The priest's grave—to the side of the church
- The holy well at the bottom of the hill

At each site prayers are recited: seven Our Father's, seven Hail Mary's, and seven Glory Be's. The final prayer is a traditional one:

> *May God and Mary bless you, O Holy Gobnait.*
> *I bless you, too, and come to you in my need.*
> *Please cure me for God's sake.*
> *Please come to my aid.*

Celebrating Saint Gobnait's Gifts to Our Lives

Saint Gobnait has indeed come to symbolize the power of enduring faith and also the larger-than-life function of faith as the foundation of a community. Gobnait was not a shy, retiring type of religious, but a stout defender of her people in good times and bad. We celebrate her as a healer, faith-seeker, and pursuer of justice.

Opening Prayer

> Saint Gobnait, pursuer of justice for people
>   who were oppressed by the powerful,
> inspire us to speak out when people suffer neglect
>   and abuse in our society.
> Give us courage to act justly and work collaboratively
>   to change systems that keep people poor
>   and marginalized in our world today.
> May we realize that we can do all things
>   by the power of the Spirit working in us.

Scripture

> "Is such the fast that I choose,
>   a day to humble oneself?
> Is it to bow down the head like a bulrush,
>   and to lie in sackcloth and ashes?
> Will you call this a fast,
>   a day acceptable to God?
> Is not this the fast that I choose:
>   to loose the bonds of injustice,
>   to undo the thongs of the yoke;
> to let the oppressed go free
>   and to break every yoke?

Is it not to share your bread with the hungry,
 and bring the homeless poor
  into your house;
when you see the naked, to cover them,
 and not to hide yourself from your own kin?
Then your light shall break forth like the dawn,
 and your healing shall spring up quickly."

ISAIAH 58:5–8

Reflection on Justice

Recall individuals, communities, and nations who suffer from poverty, disease, and discrimination. Ask God to guide you to do one activity that will serve their needs. Make a specific plan to accomplish that service.

Put prayer into action today by doing one loving thing for one of those God calls your "neighbors." Do this in the spirit of Gobnait, who was an activist when it came to serving her neighbors' needs.

Gobnait was one who listened to God's message, and then, steadfastly pursued God's instructions. Today, practice this kind of listening. Open yourself to hear what God is telling you. Use simple words of invitation: "Speak to me, my God; I am your listening servant. Guide me along the path of justice. Give me the courage to say "yes" to your call.

Intercessions

The people of Ballyvourney span the expanse of time since Gobnait's death, and come to her shrine so as to visit a present, caring friend.

Can we, in simple faith, span the years and greet Gobnait as a dear friend? Use the pilgrim's prayer with simplicity of faith, and ask God humbly, through the intercession of this holy woman, for blessings for people you know who are in need.

V.   For people who are homeless, hungry, sick, lonely, in prison, we pray.
R.   Saint Gobnait, intercede for us.

V.   For all justice advocates, we pray.
R.   Saint Gobnait, intercede for us.

V.   For people who face oppression, we pray.
R.   Saint Gobnait, intercede for us.

V.   For transformation of structures that cause injustice, we pray.
R.   Saint Gobnait, intercede for us.

V.   For two-thirds of the world who suffer from disease and poverty, we pray.
R.   Saint Gobnait, intercede for us.

V.   For an awareness of our call to be activists for justice, we pray.
R.   Saint Gobnait, intercede for us.

V.   For an integration of contemplation and action in our lives, we pray.
R.   Saint Gobnait, intercede for us.

V.   For women and men in our time who have given their lives for the needs of people who suffer injustice, especially Maura Clark, Ita Ford, Jean Donovan, Dorothy Kazel, and Bishop Oscar Romero, we pray.
R.   Saint Gobnait, intercede for us.

Closing Prayer

Saint Gobnait, open our eyes to the needs of people who face hunger, homelessness, poverty, and oppressive domination. Pray for us that we may have the courage and strength we need to lighten the load that our sisters and brothers carry. For we are the hands and feet of God on earth. Amen.

Blessing

May God, Mary, and Holy Gobnait be with us now and stay with us always. May they greet us warmly when we reach our heavenly home. Then, in the company of all the angels and saints, we will clap our hands and sing for joy with all God's family, free and whole at last from suffering and injustice. "Thank God, we are free at last!" May it be so! May it be so!

Questions for Reflection and Discussion

1. How did Gobnait exemplify a healthy balance between contemplative prayer and activist intervention? Have you struck such a balance in your spirituality?

2. How did Gobnait express a loving concern for her neighbors? Do you intervene for those you meet who have serious problems? What have you been able to accomplish for them? Thank God for the efforts and the victories? Pray for those who still need help.

3. How are you doing as a "listener" to God's instructions? Have you followed in any decisive way God's leading for your life?

4. Like Gobnait, how can you pursue justice for the oppressed?

5. Pilgrims who visit Saint Gobnait's shrine sometimes rub a piece of cloth near the cavity where Gobnait's bowl is sealed. They then put this cloth on the place that needs healing. What healing are you in need of now? Is it physical? psychological? spiritual?

CHAPTER 9

Saint Dymphna of Achill Island

SURVIVOR AND HEALER

*O God, heal me, for my bones
are shaking with terror.*
PSALM 6:2

Pilgrim Diary: Notes Along the Way

Our first stop was the Sunday liturgy at Saint Dymphna's
Church at Tydavnet which is a short distance from Monaghan
town. It was a well-attended and lively liturgy. A conversation with a parishioner led us to Ellie Sherry who knew where
Dymphna's Well was located. Ellie insisted on accompanying us to Saint Dymphna's Well—about a mile-walk through
a privately owned farm. Seventy-six-year-old Ellie amazed
us with her agility. "Oh," she said, climbing over a locked
gate and guiding us over as well, "sure I took my nitroglycerin
this morning. I'll be fine." The field where Saint Dymphna's
Well is located is filled with thistles, tall grass, and mud.

Nearby is an altar and sign marking the well and a statue of
Saint Dymphna with rags tied around her waist—apparently
items left in thanksgiving for prayers answered. Ellie informed
us that the locals do visit the well and that there used to be
sacred celebrations there, but now it is no longer a public
gathering place since the land on which it stands is in private hands.

Back at our car, and bidding our spry guide good-bye, we
drove to Cavan and then on to Lavey to visit another holy
well of Saint Dymphna. Here we met "over-eighty-year-old"
Rose Murray, who showed us the stone well located in the
middle of a river. It was raining and the walk down to the
well is a bit steep. Owen Clark, an elderly Irish man had just
driven to the well to get holy water for his ailing wife. Then
he took our water bottle and his own, walked down the in-
cline to the well, filled them, and returned, giving us ours
and carrying his up the steps to the waiting car where his
ailing wife waited. Owen was an incarnation of the deep
faith of people in the power of God's love, present to them in
the sacred water of a saint's well. What an example of the
indigenous faith that continues to pass down from generation to generation.

Saint Dymphna was a saint who traveled from place to
place, so we followed her route to Achill Island. As we ascended higher and higher on the narrow mountainous road,
sheep were grazing on the mountainside while opposite the
wild waves of the Atlantic ocean crashed against the rocks.
The drive was filled with switchbacks that got a little fright-
ening. For many miles we saw no one. Then it dawned on us:
we had taken the longer, winding coastal road. We stopped,
asked directions, and at last found our way to the hotel on
Achill Sound where we met Breege O'Brien, a young school

teacher who would be our guide and informant about all things Dymphna.

Saint Dymphna's Church, Tydavnet. Courtesy of the authors.

Encountering Saint Dymphna

According to legend Damon, Dymphna's father, was a pagan king who ruled over the kingdom of Oriel, an area covering modern-day Monaghan, Fermanagh, southern Tyrone, and part of Armagh and Louth counties. Bronagh, his wife, converted to Christianity and she raised her daughter, Dymphna, as a Christian. When Dymphna was fourteen, her mother died.

For a long time after the loss of his wife, Damon grieved and developed a serious depression. In order to help him, his servants searched the land for a woman equal to his wife. The only woman they could find to equal her was his daughter, Dymphna. Damon proposed marriage to his daughter. Shocked at the threat of incest, Dymphna fled south to Drumfurrer where she stopped and asked for a drink of water. The townsfolk refused, fearing the wrath of her father. Because of this refusal, Dymphna predicted that never would there be a well in Drumfurrer and so it is true to this day.

Dymphna and her companions crossed the Slieve Beagh Mountains and found a well on the side of the mountain at Caldavnet. This well has been a place of individual and group pilgrimage through the centuries.

In Tydavnet, Dymphna asked the village blacksmith for coals to light a fire. She had no container to hold them but offered her apron. According to the legend, he placed the coals in her apron and they did not burn through.

The fugitives stayed in Tydavnet in a house where Dymphna performed a miracle. This feat accounts for the name of the town: *tigh* meaning "house" and *davnet* meaning "Dymphna." To commemorate her stay in this village, a church was founded which became the burial place of the kings of Oriel.

Then, according to folklore, Dymphna went to the village of Lavey in County Cavan. In Lavey, one of the oldest church sites is dedicated to Saint Dymphna. Nearby are Dymphna's Stone which once bore the imprint of her knees and the Holy Pool where the footprints of an unshod colt are visible on the stones of the riverbed. This is said to be the colt that carried Dymphna across the water westwards to Achill and Kildavnet.

Dymphna's stay in Achill did not last long. She fled Ireland from the west coast when her father's soldiers followed her to the island. The travelers escaped to Antwerp and found a hiding place at Zammel near Geel, a small town southeast of Antwerp. Here they erected dwellings for themselves close to the ruins of a monastery dedicated to Saint Martin of Tours.

Damon kept up his pursuit until he found Dymphna and when she again refused his demands, he had her companion Genebern beheaded. He then beheaded his own daughter. In that instant, Damon's insane lust for his daughter was healed. Some local people in Geel buried the bodies of the martyrs in a cave.

Later, when the bodies were exhumed to be buried in a church, they were found in two white coffins made of stone that was not native to the area. As a result, the story circulated that they were buried by angels. The relics were moved to a church dedicated to Saint Dymphna and devotion to the saint begun. People began to bring mentally ill family members to this site, and soon word spread that people who were mentally ill were being cured at Dymphna's grave. Gradually, a home was built for them, and, in 1286, a hospital was founded at Geel for the care of the mentally ill. For this reason, Saint Dymphna is known as patron of people suffering from mental illness, depression, and epilepsy.

In 1349, a new church was constructed to accommodate the large number of pilgrimages to the site. These pilgrimages consisted of a novena, nine days of prayer and penance. Afterwards, some pilgrims remained in the homes of Geel families. This practice of family care for people with mental sickness became known as "the Geel system" of psychiatric care. A Geel family became a foster family, adopting a patient and providing room and board. The patients participated in the usual activities of the town. In 1936, a U.S. doctor, Charles D. Aring, visited Geel and is quoted in Breege O'Brien's article in the *Achill Island Journal* as saying: "A twelve-year-old girl, with a younger brother in her charge, was also caring for two patients while her parents were in town or in the fields. She was not perturbed in the least by our visit. With consummate consideration, she presented her charges. The children of the village learned by experience and tradition that mental disease is neither fearful nor amusing and, like their parents, became skilled in the art of caring for the mentally ill."

Our primary source for the legends and places associated with Saint Dymphna is Breege O'Brien's series of articles on the "Legacy of Saint Dymphna." We are indebted to her for her articles, interviews, and tour. (This material is based on her extensive research and used with her kind permission.)

Some scholars think that the Saint Dymphna of Achill and Dymphna of Geel were not the same person. A point they make to support this contention is that if Dymphna had crossed the sea from Ireland, she would not have come in through Antwerp since it was not on a direct route from Ireland. Second, they consider the evidence of the crozier of Saint Dymphna that is displayed in the museum in Dublin and argue that the crozier is a symbol of a church leader and, therefore, if Saint Dymphna founded a church in Ireland, she more than likely would have stayed in Ireland. Scholars also point out that the story of Saint Dymphna of Geel may have come from a European folk tradition that portrayed the recurring theme of the incestuous father who pursued an illegitimate relationship with his daughter. Still, there is a strong tradition that Saint Dymphna of Achill and Geel were the same woman.

Saint Dymphna's site in Kildavnet is located in the gently sloping hills of the southeastern shore of Achill Island. The site around the unroofed church was restored in recent years.

For centuries, this church was the only church in Achill. There are stories of people coming from all over the island carrying coffins to bury their dead in this cemetery. People still stop here for quiet prayer, and many attend an annual Mass at the site.

The well is situated on the shore of the bay near this church and cemetery and is sometimes covered with the tide. However it is a fresh-water well. The traditional "pattern," the practice of saying prayers while walking around a holy site or well several times, was popular at Saint Dymphna's site at Kildavnet. According to Breege O'Brien, pilgrims at Saint Dymphna's Well walk around the well in a circular pattern reciting seven Hail Marys each time. Each time they drop a stone in the well and bow three times at intervals to acknowledge *Tobar Ri an Domhnaigh* (The Well of the King and Dymphna). Then the pilgrims take water from the well. If they should see a fish in the water, this could indicate good luck, marriage, or a death in the family, depending on the way the fish was lying. They would leave a lock of their hair or a piece of their clothing at the well in thanksgiving for a healing or blessing received.

Celebrating Saint Dymphna's Gifts for Our Lives

Breege O'Brien sees certain patterns emerging from the life of Dymphna which speak to today's society:

1. Kind outreach to those who are rejected by society such as mentally ill.
2. Adherence to ideals in spite of persecution.
3. The triumph of female integrity over male sexual violence.

Certainly, the story of Dymphna speaks to people suffering any kind of sexual abuse, sexual insecurity, or any kind of sexual issue. Her life speaks to fathers and children and spouses. In Ireland today the church has been devastated with stories of sexual abuse. Professor Conor K. Ward of the National University of Ireland and U. S. sociologist Andrew Greeley conducted two surveys of the Republic of Ireland in 1991 and 1998. Greeley summarizes their findings: "If the proper measures of Catholicism are faith and devotion, then the Irish are still Catholic. There has been no change in their belief in God, heaven, miracles and life after death in the last decade, and church attendance rates are still the highest in Europe (and have not declined either). Sixty-three percent attend Mass once a week and seventy-three percent two or three times a month. If, on the other hand, the proper measures of faith are acceptance of church authority and adherence to the church's sexual and reproductive ethic, then the Irish are no longer Catholic....Only thirty percent think that premarital sex is always wrong, and sixty percent that same-sex relations are always wrong. Confidence in the church organization has fallen from forty-six percent in 1991 to twenty-seven percent in 1998, and the feeling that the Church has too much power has increased from thirty-eight percent to forty-six percent." (Source: Andrew Greeley, "Religion in the Emerald Tiger," *America*, March 12, 2001.)

The story of Saint Dymphna is a story of good coming out of evil. As she fled her father's pursuit, Dymphna was a refugee. Hundreds of thousands of people around the world are or have been refugees—homeless, stranded, on the move, at the mercy of strangers and nature. Where is God, we may ask in such circumstances. The legend of Dymphna is a faith story of a belief that endures through the ages. God is our refuge. God is our home. Ultimately, we have nothing to fear, even death itself is not the last word. God will not abandon us. We can find a safe place, our home, in God who dwells with us. That certainly does not imply that we should take on a victim mentality and allow people to abuse or mistreat us. Dymphna removed herself from a situation that would violate her integrity, but, like millions of women throughout history, she died as a victim of violence. Her story should be a source of hope for us. In our darkest hour, no matter what happens to us, God is beside us. When we are in need, alone, and in pain, God is near. At the moment of Dymphna's death, God's healing love flowed through her, and her father was cured. God can bless all the disasters of life and bring good out of the most tragic circumstances. Corrie Ten Boom, a victim of the Nazi concentration camp, once said "There is no pit so deep that God's love is not deeper still."

Many people in today's world face the stresses, anxieties, and pressures of mortgages, unpaid bills, and children to raise. They experience a life full of complexities, challenges, and chaos. Where do we go for consolation? One approach is to realize that no matter what happens God is at home in us and with us. We can find our home, our peace, in God who walks with us, weeps with us, laughs with us, works with and through us and leads us to find the goodness that is often hidden beneath the rubble of broken relationships and the pressures of ordinary living.

The next time, you are exasperated with someone, picture God sitting with you and listening to your conversation. Then ask yourself, how you should handle the relationship problem?

Celebrating Saint Dymphna's Gifts for Our Lives

In Dymphna's life she brought peace and healing to those she encountered. She reached out to those she met on her way, blessing people who helped her and, in the last analysis, healing her father's insanity. Let us celebrate this healer who can bring us release from emotional pain.

Opening Prayer

Saint Dymphna, object of abuse, you who knew fear and fled the incestuous demands of your Father, be anam chara, *be a soul-friend, to women who experience rape, violence, and abuse, especially at the hands of family members. Accompany them on their journey to freedom, empowerment, forgiveness, and wholeness. Amen.*

Scripture

Have mercy on me, O God, have mercy on me!
    In you my soul takes shelter;
I take shelter in the shadow of your wings
    until the destroying storm is over.
I call on God the Most High,
    on God who has done everything for me,
to send help from heaven to save me,
to stop them from persecuting me.

O God, send me your love
    and your faithfulness....
They laid a net where I was walking
    when I was bowed with care;
they dug a pit for me
    but fell into it themselves.

My heart is ready, O God,
    my heart is ready;
I will sing and play for you....
I will thank you among the peoples, Adonai,
    and sing of you among the nations;
your love is high as heaven,
    your faithfulness reaches to the skies.

                        PSALM 57 (*INCLUSIVE PSALMS*)

Meditation and Reflection

We begin our prayerful reflection on sexual wholeness by
becoming aware of our breath. As you breathe in and out,
relax your body. Breathe deeply and rhythmically through
your nose so that your abdomen rises as you inhale and low-
ers as you exhale through your mouth.

Become aware of your sexuality. Affirm your body-spirit
as the beautiful creation of the Holy One. Remember the
loving relationships that helped you grow more aware of your
own goodness, tenderness, and passion. Reflect on treasured
memories of loving and being loved. Allow the memory of
love and friendship to speak to your heart.

If you become conscious of any negative memories of
sexual abuse or violation that you experienced or a loved
one experienced be aware that God can heal past wounds.
Invite the Divine Healer to embrace you and love you through
your pain for as long as you need the special support. (This
process may be repeated over and over until God's love heals
and transforms the memory of your hurt. If this experience
becomes too intense, turn to an experienced counselor or
spiritual director to work out your feelings.)

Be aware that God is at home in you. Your body is holy.
You are God's favorite dwelling place. Pray for women who

have suffered any form of abuse or violent assault. See yourself as a "healing balm," an instrument of healing, a resource for life and empowerment for all those in need of encouragement and hope. Let us join hands and hearts in an act of spiritual solidarity with women survivors, our sisters and friends.

Gently recall God's word to you. Say your name followed by "Peace I leave with you, / my peace I give to you; / but the kind of peace I give you / is not like the world's peace. / Don't let your hearts be distressed; / don't be fearful" (Jn 14:27, *Inclusive New Testament*).

Intercessions

V. When we struggle with issues of abuse and violence in our families and in our world, we pray.

R. Jesus, give us your peace.

V. When we are weary with illness of body or mind, we pray.

R. Jesus, give us your peace.

V. When we are with others who suffer physical or mental illnesses, we pray.

R. Jesus, give us your peace.

V. When we feel discouraged and lonely and want to give up, we pray.

R. Jesus, give us your peace.

V. When we experience worry and anxiety, we pray.

R. Jesus, give us your peace.

V. When we find it hard to let go of old resentments and still hold grudges, we pray.

R. Jesus, give us your peace.

V. When we have too much to do and are stressed out, we pray.
R. Jesus, give us your peace.

V. When we have no where to turn and are at the end of our rope, we pray.
R. Jesus, give us your peace.

V. When we face staggering bills, relationship problems, and job insecurities, we pray.
R. Jesus, give us your peace.

V. When we are grieving for loss of a loved one, we pray.
R. Jesus, give us your peace.

V. When we are dealing with sexuality issues, we pray.
R. Jesus, give us your peace.

V. When we are resistant to growth in our relationships, we pray.
R. Jesus, give us your peace.

Blessing Prayer

Gather in a circle. Extend your arm in blessing to the person on your right, place your hand on his or her shoulder or join hands. Then this person turns to you and prays for several minutes in silence. During this time of prayer, you may want to play soft instrumental music in the background.

Begin by praying for several minutes in silence for the person to your right. As you pray, be aware that you are an instrument of God's healing compassion to the person you are praying with, let divine love flow through you and heal whatever God wants to touch in this person this day.

After this blessing prayer, offer a handshake, a bow, or a

hug to the person(s) and/or group with whom you have prayed as a sign of peace.

Questions for Reflection and Discussion

1. What is the meaning of the story of Saint Dymphna for women survivors of sexual/violent assault?
2. What can we do to address issues of sexual abuse in our society? What concrete steps can be taken by me to counter these prevailing attitudes and actions?
3. How can we affirm the goodness of our sexuality?
4. If we believe God is our home, and that we are God's favorite dwelling place, what difference does it make when we encounter people who reject or attack us?
5. Invite God to sit down with you for a cup of tea or coffee. What would you say? What advice would you listen for?

CHAPTER 10

Saint Samthann of Clonbroney

WISE SOUL FRIEND

Seek advice from every wise person and do not despise any useful counsel. At all times bless…God, and ask…that your ways may be made straight and that all your paths and plans may prosper.

TOBIT 4:18–19

Pilgrim Diary: Notes Along the Way

We knew that the ruins of Saint Samthann's monastery were located in the Parish of Clonbroney (or Cluain Bronaigh, the field of Bronaigh), near the town of Ballinalee, in County Longford, though we did not know the monastery's exact location. We drove around unsuccessfully for an hour and finally found the parish church. When we went inside, it was obvious that this was not the ancient site, for nothing there gave a clue about Saint Samthann. We continued on our journey, stopping and asking directions of people along the way. Finally, someone told us that we needed to go to "old Clonbroney." After about twenty minutes of further driving, a friendly Irishman led us to the turnoff for "old Clonbroney."

We followed the road and wound up at what appeared to be a dead end where the narrow (as in no room for another car to pass) road ended at a wooded clearing. With great difficulty, we turned around, grateful not to have wound up in the ditch. As we drove back up the road, we noticed a stone wall and an overgrown cemetery. We stopped and, as we got out of the car, a dog from a nearby farm came out barking a greeting. Then the local farmer, John O'Reilly, following his dog's lead, came down the lane to us and introduced himself. He assured us that we had reached the site of Saint Samthann's monastic foundation. He gave us the history of the ancient site and then invited us into his home where we met his family.

After tea and answering many of our questions, the O'Reilly family gave us an excellent resource entitled *Clonbroney With Ballinalee: A Local History*. As it turns out, John is a retired tour bus driver who had great familiarity with the local sights. He provided us with easy-to-follow directions to our next destination, the Knock shrine in County Mayo. In our estimation, getting lost on a pilgrimage can be a great blessing that leads us to people and places that we may never have found otherwise. After this adventure we now know that Clonbroney is located three-quarters of a mile off the Ballinalee/Granard Road near the southwestern corner of Clonfin Lough.

According to "Life of Saint Samthann," which can be found in manuscript form at the Bodleian Library at Oxford University, Abbess Fuinech was the founder of the monastery of

Clonbroney. It was here that Saint Patrick is said to have given the veil to the two Emers, sisters of Gusacht, who Saint Patrick had installed as abbesses of Granard. Anlaith, who died in 933 A.D., was abbess of Clonbroney and Cloonburren (County Roscommon). According to Hadcock and Gwynn's *Medieval Religious Houses of Ireland*, the convents of Cloonburren, Kildare, and Clonbroney continued to be prominent communities of women for several centuries, emphasizing the importance of women as leaders in the earliest Irish monastic foundations. Kildare was established by Brigit in the fifth century, Killeevy in Armagh by Monenna near the end of the fifth century, Killeedy in County Limerick by Ita around 550 A.D., Ballyvourney by Gobnait in the seventh century, and Clonbroney in County Longford by Samthann in the seventh century.

According to Ann Donohoe's local history *Clonbroney With Ballinalee* (1977), after the Normans invaded, the parish church in Clonbroney was transferred to Moatfarrell, but the ancient cemetery continued to be a burying place up to modern times and became known as "old Clonbroney."

Encountering Saint Samthann

Samthann, also known as Safan, was born in Ulster. Her father was Diamramus and her mother was Columba. Cridan, her foster father, who was king of Ireland, promised Samthann in marriage to a nobleman. Apparently, Samthann did not have much of a choice in the matter, so on her wedding night, she prayed and a fire flamed from her mouth to the roof of the house. Before the fire could destroy the town, it was extinguished. Samthann went into hiding, but when Cridan found her, he agreed to let her decide. Samthann said,

"This is my decision: as of now you give me as a spouse to God and not to man." Then, with the agreement of her husband she entered the monastery and was later appointed abbess of Clonbroney by the foundress Fuinech.

A wise *anam chara*, or soul friend, Samthann gave sound spiritual advice that has endured the test of time. Once a monk inquired which is the most appropriate position for prayer, standing, sitting, or lying prostrate. She replied "each and all of them." To a teacher who shared his desire to leave aside his studies in order to dedicate his life to prayer, she challenged, "How will you ever be able to learn to concentrate in prayer if you can't even keep your mind on your books?"

The teacher then asked her about the spiritual benefits of undertaking a pilgrimage. She answered in what appears to be a tongue-in-cheek reply, "If God cannot be found on this side of the sea, by all means journey overseas, but since God is near to all who call on God, there is no need to cross the sea. The kingdom of God can be reached from every land."

Samthann was reported to be the confessor or *anam chara* of Maelruain, one of the *Celi De* movement's leader. According to Richard J. Woods, the *Celi De* was a seventh-century reform movement dedicated to revitalizing Celtic spirituality. "Their chief contribution," observes Richard Woods, "was a determined spirituality that, in resisting the increasing secularization of the monasteries, married monks, and strife between rival monasteries, returned to the austere spirit of the founding saints of centuries past" (Richard J. Woods, *The Spirituality of the Celtic Saints*, Maryknoll, New York: Orbis, 2000).

One day, an itinerant messenger from Samthann asked Maelruain if he would accept women as soul friends and if he would agree to have Samthann as an *anam chara*. His response to her was that he would certainly seek spiritual advice from her.

Samthann, like Brigit of Kildare, had a reputation for compassion and generous giving. It is said that she shared her food and alms with her sisters and with people who were poor and in need. On one occasion, a leper was stranded across a pond. Samthann and her companions picked him up and brought him across in their boat. Then she supplied the leper with food and clothing to meet his needs.

One day, Niall, son of King Fergall, asked for the staff of Samthann to adorn with gold and silver. But the staff was so crooked and old, he could not achieve his purpose. The crozier was then placed over the king's bed. During the night, by a miracle, the wood was transformed into a beautiful work of art.

On the night of her death, Saint Samthann appeared before Abbot Laserian in the form of a star. He bade her farewell in these words: "Well done, faithful servant of God, Samthann, because you are now about to enter the joy of your Lord and Spouse." Saint Samthann died in 739 A.D. Her feast is celebrated on December 19. She is invoked in both the litany and canon of the Stowe Missal.

Celebrating Saint Samthann's Gifts for Our Lives

Samthann was a wise woman, a woman of prayer, who held strongly to the divine mercy of God. Though devotion to Samthann was introduced into the continent by Saint Virgilius of Salzburg, Samthann is a guiding light of Celtic soul-friend customs and her example can continue to inspire and guide us. Here we appreciate her for her many contributions.

Opening Prayer

God of My Yearning,
You speak to me
in the depths of my soul
of love beyond all telling.
Guide me to unravel
the epiphanies of grace
and wonders of your life
on my earthly journey.
May I be blessed to have an anam chara,
like Saint Samthann,
with whom I can share
my heart's deep yearnings and
who can shepherd my growth in wisdom.
Let it be. Let it be. Amen.

Scriptures

"A student is not superior to the teacher; the follower is not above the leader. The student should be glad simply to become like the teacher, the follower like the leader.

"If the head of the house has been called Beelzebul, how much more the members of the household!

"Don't let people intimidate you. Nothing is concealed that will not be revealed, and nothing is hidden that will not be made known. What I tell you in darkness, speak in the light. What you hear in private, proclaim from the housetops."

MATTHEW 10:24–27 (*INCLUSIVE NEW TESTAMENT*)

Meditation and Reflection

Start your reflection by playing gentle instrumental music as background for your meditation. Begin by becoming aware of your breath. As you breathe in and as you breathe out, imagine that with each breath, you begin to release any tension you may have. As you relax more deeply, your mind and body become calm and peaceful. When you feel ready, go to your heart's deep center where you are at home in God's presence.

Open yourself to the infinite, tender, expressive love of God for you. Listen as God calls you by name and sings for joy for your presence. Realize that you are God's beloved child. You are precious. You are loved beyond your wildest imaginings.

What do you see? What do you hear? When you find this loving state, take note of what you see, of what you hear.

Repeat one of the following short prayers or mantras to remind you of God's love, make up one of your own, or choose one that the Spirit has whispered in your soul.

- *I am God's beloved.*
- *God delights in me.*
- *God sings for joy over me.*
- *I am a glorious image of the Holy One.*
- *I rest calmly in the assurance of God's love.*

Reflect on your spiritual journey over the different ages and stages of your life: child, teen, young adult, mature adult. How would you describe the sacred in your life? Who was God for you? Divine Parent? Friend? Savior? Lover? At what stage of life was God most present? Where is God leading you now?

Be aware of any thoughts, images, or feelings that emerge as you reflect on these questions. You may want to write them in a journal for further reflection or for sharing with a spiritual friend at a later time.

Imagine yourself sharing your sacred journey with a spiritual friend or *anam chara* as you share a meal together. Take some time to have a long chat. What did you learn that can lead you to deeper wisdom?

Make a decision to share this experience with your *anam chara* or if you don't have an *anam chara*, think about entering into a spiritual friendship relationship with a person you trust.

Go now in joy and peace aware always that you are the beloved of God.

Closing Prayer

> The encompassing of God be on you and on me,
>   the encompassing of the God of life.
> The encompassing of Christ be on you and on me,
>   the encompassing of the Christ of love.
> The encompassing of the Spirit be on you and on me,
>   the encompassing of the Spirit of Grace.
> The encompassing of the Three be on you and on me.
> The encompassing of the Three preserve you and me.
>
> ADAPTED FROM ALEXANDER CARMICHAEL'S *CARMINA GADELICA*

A Blessing for All Your Kin

> May the fire of God's love warm your hearts.
> May God grant your prayers of healing
>   for the broken and the wounded.
> May the Love of Christ be in your hearts for everyone.
> May the road rise to meet you.
>   May the wind be always at your back.
>   May the sun shine warm upon your face.
>   And the rain fall soft upon your fields.
>   And until we meet again,
>   May you be held in the palm of God's hand.
>
> OLD IRISH BLESSING

Questions for Reflection and Discussion

1. Do you believe that God rejoices over you? How can you receive affirmations from the heart of God? What further can you do to become aware of this positive and accepting love from God?

2. Why is it a spiritual benefit to have an *anam chara*, or soul friend? Do you know of any spiritual mentors of your own acquaintance? What have been some of the famous spiritual friendships throughout history?

3. What can contemporary spiritual seekers learn from Saint Samthann? How can we emulate Samthann's generosity? How can we emulate Samthann's compassion? How can we emulate her persistence in following her own goal to be a nun instead of a wife?

4. How can you live more fully and joyfully in God's love now? What would it take to accomplish this?

5. It is said that Saint Samthann refused large donations to her monastery for fear of losing the simplicity and spirituality of their lives. What can we "refuse" in order to protect our own spiritual practice?

The Stowe Missal, a translation from Latin and Gaelic, reflects a true Celtic form of the liturgy from before 650 A.D. Above is a detail from the Litany of the Saints which includes Saint Samthann in its listing.

Detail from the Book of Kells

mary of Nazareth

OUR BLESSED MOTHER

Six months later, the angel Gabriel was sent from God to a town in Galilee called Nazareth, to a young woman named Mary; she was engaged to a man named Joseph, of the house of David. Upon arriving, the angel said to Mary, "Rejoice, highly favored one! God is with you! Blessed are you among women!"

Mary was deeply troubled by these words and wondered what the angel's greeting meant. The angel went on to say to her, "Don't be afraid, Mary. You have found favor with God. You'll conceive and bear a son, and give him the name Jesus—'Deliverance.' His dignity will be great, and he will be called the Only Begotten of God. God will give Jesus the judgment seat of David, his ancestor, to rule over the house of Jacob forever, and his reign will never end."

LUKE 1:26–33 (*INCLUSIVE NEW TESTAMENT*)

Pilgrim Diary: Notes Along the Way

Primary among Ireland's Marian shrines is Knock, which also has become one of the world's major Marian shrines. Knock is often called the "Lourdes of Ireland."

A steady stream of pilgrims came into the beautiful, newly renovated Apparition Gable chapel the day we were there in September 2000. This chapel marks the spot where Mary, Saint Joseph, and Saint John are reported to have appeared on the church wall in 1879. To their right, and in the middle of the church wall, was a plain altar on which was standing a lamb—the symbol of Jesus. A group of angels hovered about the lamb. This apparition has been documented by interviews with the fifteen people who saw it.

We watched as small groups of pilgrims, reciting the rosary, walked around this chapel in the ancient tradition of "doing the pattern," that is, walking sun-wise around a shrine or holy well, reciting certain prescribed prayers. Like the invisible Irish mist that often falls gently on this Emerald Isle, peace and serenity seemed to permeate everyone and everything at Mary's shrine. It felt good to be there in that powerful atmosphere of prayer and simplicity of faith! Masses were held on the hour, and the Reconciliation Chapel was open all day.

Although there is no holy well at Knock, there are faucets by the wall near the gate which contain holy water; and pilgrims come to fill up their bottles to carry home to family and friends. It is a custom in many Irish families to keep holy water in the house. Some homes still have holy water fonts at the door. In the Meehan's cottage in Ireland and in their home in the United States, there is a holy water font near the front door to remind the family of God's nearness in their comings and goings.

Pilgrims through the years have touched a spot on the sidewall of the church which they believed was the place that Our Lady appeared. We were greatly moved as we watched older women and men stop and kiss this spot. Monsignor Dominick Grealy, in his booklet on Knock, *The Apparition Gable*, notes that shrine officials have now encased in the front wall of the new shrine enclosure an authentic section of the original Apparition Gable which pilgrims may touch if they wish.

On a number of earlier visits to Ireland, Bridget had visited Knock with her family and relatives. Her mother, Bridie, had a very close relationship with the Blessed Mother and inculcated that devotion in her children from their earliest years. One of Bridget's first memories is every evening kneeling by the couch next to her brothers Patrick and Sean, as her mother led the family in the rosary. It always ended with "the trimmings," that is, the litany to the Blessed Mother and the invocation: "O Mary, conceived without sin; pray for us who have recourse to you." So when Bridget's family spent holidays in Ireland, Knock was a favorite stop. After a time of prayer, they always stocked up on holy water for the year.

About ten years ago, Regina and Bridget accompanied Bridget's Aunt Molly and a group from Portleix on a pilgrimage to Knock. This was our first experience of an "Irish style pilgrimage." On the bus trip to and from Knock, the group recited the fifteen decades of the rosary twice. Once there, the pilgrims did the "pattern" around the stations and the apparition chapel, filled holy water bottles, received the sacrament of reconciliation, and attended Mass at the basilica. It was quite a spiritual workout even for two nuns!

Encountering Our Lady of Knock

At eight o'clock on a rainy Thursday on August 21, 1879, fifteen people of different ages witnessed the apparition of Our Lady, Saint Joseph, and Saint John the Evangelist on the south gable of the Church of Knock.

Mary Byrne and her brother Dominick Byrne, young people who lived in the village of Knock, were eyewitnesses to the heavenly apparition. Their descriptions of the apparition are recorded in a book titled *I Saw Our Lady*, published by the Custodians of Knock Shrine, 1995.

Mary was about three hundred yards from the church when, according to her testimony, "I beheld, all at once, standing out from the gable, and rather to the west of it, three figures which on more attentive inspection, appeared to be that of the Blessed Virgin, Saint Joseph, and Saint John. The Virgin stood erect, with eyes raised to heaven, her hands elevated to the shoulders or a little higher, the palms inclined slightly towards the shoulders or bosom. She wore a crown on the head, rather a large crown and it appeared to me somewhat yellower than the dress or robes worn by Our Blessed Lady."

Dominick Byrne, her brother and also an eyewitness, described the figures as life-sized, and standing about a foot from the ground, looking like statues. "The Blessed Virgin was in the middle. Her face was turned out to us. Her eyes were lifted up, in the manner of praying….Saint Joseph was on her right-hand side, and turned towards her. His hands were joined together, and he was stooping. His hair and beard looked gray. On the left side was Saint John. He was dressed in a long robe and had on a miter. He was turned partly out, and partly away from the Blessed Virgin facing an altar farther on to the left-hand side of the gable. On his left hand he was holding a large book open. His right arm was lifted up in the form of blessing."

Beside the heavenly figures and to the right, in the center of the gable was a plain altar on which stood a lamb around which angels hovered. Behind the lamb there was a large cross. The vision remained for two hours, during which time the people present prayed the rosary. Two Commissions of Inquiry, one in 1897 and one in 1936, found that their testimony of the witnesses was trustworthy.

Almost immediately, numerous healings were achieved as a result of devotion to Our Lady of Knock. Here are some of the first healings reported in a newspaper in September 1880 and recorded in Tom Neary's *I Saw Our Lady*.

Thomas McCann was crippled for twenty-two years. His right leg could not be straightened or bent, and he could not move without a crutch. One day he went to the priest's house, applied some water from the shrine on his leg, and, upon arriving at the church, felt a strange sensation in his leg. The coldness in his leg was gone, and he left his crutch at the church and walked about a half-mile to his home.

Twenty-nine-year-old Margaret Doyle of Gull Island suffered from severe asthma attacks for eight years. The doctors gave up on her, and she had received the last sacraments. Father Hanley, the parish priest, gave her a small quantity of water with a few particles of the cement from the chapel of Knock. After the first application of the water, she was completely cured. She reported that the following Sunday she had been able to walk to Mass. Since then she never had any more symptoms.

Patrick Hogan complained of gradually losing his eyesight. It got to the stage in which he could not see objects eight hundred yards away. After applying Knock water to his eyes, the film left his eyes and he could see a lighthouse a great distance away for the first time.

In order to understand the significance of the apparition of Our Lady of Knock, it is important to place it in its historical context. In his presentation of the background of Knock, Tom Neary reminds the reader that the West of Ireland was a place of dire poverty and homelessness in the late nineteenth century. It was a time of hunger, famine, emigration. One Englishman noted the sad state of affairs on his travels through Galway and Mayo: "Rents cannot be paid while there is nothing to be earned and when evictions abound, as they threaten to abound, we shall hear that scores of families are living or dying in "dens and caves of the earth."

In her book *Women of the Celts* (Rochester, Vermont: Inner Traditions, 1986), Jean Markale notes a resemblance between devotion to Mary and the traditions associated with Celtic goddesses. In fact on the site where the Chartres Cathedral stands in France is an underground sanctuary in which stands a statue of a mother-goddess. The shrine is referred to as "Our Lady Under the Ground."

Celtic holy women were virgins, but at the same time, they were symbolic mothers, responsible for the well-being of their people and lands. Miranda Green, in her work *Celtic Goddesses*, points out that Mary was a virgin when she became mother of Jesus and she was also a disciple of her son. The Celtic goddess, Arianrod, was also known as a virgin and mother and presents a parallel. The legend further portrays Arianrod's son, Lleu, as reaching a greater status than his mother had attained.

Devotion to Mary is as natural and comfortable for the Celtic soul as the fresh air that blows across the Cliffs of

Moher on the coast of County Clare. Although not divine herself, Mary is the most powerful icon or image by which we can experience the mothering side of God. The Celtic soul has cherished the feminine face of divinity from ancient times. Later, when the Celts embraced Christianity, attributes of the goddesses were transferred to the Blessed Mother and the women saints. Quite simply, for centuries Mary has reflected the loving heart of a mothering God who is nurturer, comforter, and healer. This is the Mary we meet at shrines such as Our Lady of Knock. Mary, our universal mother, is a reminder that God's tender warm love always embraces us.

Celebrating the Gifts of Our Lady for Our Lives

By her appearance at Knock, Mary reminds the Irish people and us that God is with them, that God will heal them, that God sees their oppression and will be their vindicator. The promises God made to the Hebrew people long ago are the same promises that God makes to the people in the destitute, poverty-stricken West of Ireland. God will provide a way out. God will raise up courageous men and women who set Ireland free and restore dignity to all her children. God sends Mary as a sign of mercy and hope in a time of darkness and despair. In the end, the people who witnessed the apparition who knew, and all the people of Ireland knew as well, that Mary's visit meant all would be well because they were experiencing God's intervention, assuring them that they were God's beloved people, who one day live in freedom, dignity and prosperity. As the passage in Luke reminds us: The mercy of the Compassionate One reaches from age to age.

Opening Prayer

Mary, Blessed Mother,
Reflection of God's warm mothering love,
embrace us this day
with the strength, peace, and healing we need
to reflect the presence of the Holy One in our world.
May we be prophetic voices for people of the world
    who suffer poverty, hunger and oppression,
assuring them that they are God's beloved people.
May we work for justice and peace around the globe.

> *Flower-garland of the ocean,*
> *Flower-garland of the land,*
> *Flower-garland of the heavens,*
> *Mary, Mother of God,*
> *We praise you, we thank you, we love you.*
>
> *Flower-garland of the earth,*
> *Flower-garland of the skies,*
> *Flower-garland of the angels,*
> *Mary, Mother of God,*
> *We praise you, we thank you, we love you.*
>
> *Flower-garland of the mansion,*
> *Flower-garland of the stars,*
> *Flower-garland of paradise,*
> *Mary, Mother of God,*
> *We praise you, we thank you, we love you.*

ADAPTED FROM ALEXANDER CARMICHAEL'S
CARMINA GADELICA

Scripture

Within a few days Mary set out and hurried to the hill country to a town of Judah, where she entered Zechariah's house and greeted Elizabeth.

As soon as Elizabeth heard Mary's greeting, the child leaped in her womb and Elizabeth was filled with the Holy Spirit. In a loud voice she exclaimed, "Blessed are you among women, and blessed is the fruit of your womb! But why am I so favored, that the mother of the Messiah should come to me? The moment your greeting reached my ears, the child in my womb leaped for joy. Blessed is she who believed that what Our God said to her would be accomplished!"

Mary said:

"My soul proclaims your greatness, O God,
    and my spirit rejoices in you, my Savior.
For you have looked with favor
    upon your lowly servant,
and from this day forward
    all generations will call me blessed.
For you, the Almighty, have done great things for
me, and holy is your Name.
Your mercy reaches from age to age
    for those who fear you.
You have shown strength with your arm,
    you have scattered the proud in their conceit,
you have deposed the mighty from their thrones
    and raised the lowly to high places.
You have filled the hungry with good things,
    while you sent the rich away empty.
    You have come to the aid of Israel your servant,
        mindful of your mercy—

the promise made to our ancestors—
to Sarah and Abraham
and their descendants forever."
Mary stayed with Elizabeth about three months and then
returned home.

LUKE 1:39-56 (*INCLUSIVE NEW TESTAMENT*)

Meditation and Reflection

In her book *The Friendship of Women* (Erie, Pennsylvania:
Benetvision, 2000), Joan Chittister reflects on the friendship
between Mary and Elizabeth: "The Elizabeth factor in friendship is a fierce commitment to hold on with hope to the spiritual fecundity of a friend. However dark, however debilitating,
the circumstances with which the friend may be grappling at
the moment, Elizabeth knows that in the end will come goodness because goodness is of the essence of the one we love as
we love ourselves. Acceptance is the universal currency of
real friendship. It allows the other to be the other. It puts no
barriers where life should be. It does not warp or shape or
wrench a person to be anything other than what they are. It
simply opens its arms to hold the weary and opens its heart
to hear the broken and opens its mind to see the invisible.
Then, in the shelter of acceptance, a person can be free to be
even something more."

Reflect on times in your life when you experienced the
acceptance of genuine friendship—times when you saw your
own goodness reflected through the eyes of a friend. Be aware
of any feelings or images that arise in you. Give thanks for
each friend who has given you the gift of acceptance.

Reflect on times in your life when you held friends or a
friend in your arms or heart and you reflected their goodness
back to them, especially when they were discouraged, afraid,

weary, or lonely, when you offered warmth, love, and companionship to them. Be aware of any feelings or images that arise in you. Give thanks for each memory.

Reflect on Mary as an image of a mothering God, affirming you as an image of divine goodness, holding your "spiritual fecundity," encouraging you to grow spiritually. See yourself becoming "something more." Be aware of any feelings or images that arise in you. Give thanks for each insight.

Imagine yourself as an image of a mothering person, holding, accepting, nurturing, supporting, and comforting people who are neglected, rejected, wounded, in need of a real friend. Be aware of any feelings or images that arise in you. Give thanks for each insight.

Intercessions

V. Console people who are lonely and grieving.

R. Mother of God, love through us.

V. Free those burdened with guilt.

R. Mother of God, love through us.

V. Heal the sick, especially those heavily burdened this day (*name individuals or groups needing special help*).

R. Mother of God, love through us.

V. Fill the hungry, shelter the homeless.

R. Mother of God, love through us.

V. Strengthen people who feel disempowered.

R. Mother of God, love through us.

V. Deliver abusers from abusing others.

R. Mother of God, love through us.

V. Calm those who worry.
R. Mother of God, love through us.

V. Encourage the despairing.
R. Mother of God, love through us.

V. Guide those who are lost.
R. Mother of God, love through us.

V. Give wisdom to those who are confused.
R. Mother of God, love through us.

V. Transform unjust structures that oppress and dominate peoples and nations.
R. Mother of God, love through us.

Closing Prayer

Our Lady of Knock,
Brighter than worlds of sunbursts beaming,
Fairer than myriads of fair stars gleaming,
Whiter than floods of moon waves streaming,
Vision of love, of a pure heart's dealing,
Our Lady of Knock, pray for us.

Thy beauty the heavens and earth transcending,
Purer than crystalline dews descending
On the lips of the rose low bending,
Softer than rays of the rainbow blending,
Sweeter than incense clouds ascending,
Our Lady of Knock, pray for us.

In your charms more wonders combining
Than the mightiest mind in its art defining,
Fairer than milk-white lilies entwining,
Their petals of gold round their heart's own lining.

Far above mortals' or angels' divining
Our Lady of Knock, pray for us.

"Queen of all queens" bespeaks thy brow,
Virgin of Virgins, we fervently vow
To thy service each day that our lives will allow.
Life of our Life! To thee we bow.
Joy of our joy! We hail thee now;
Our Lady of Knock, pray for us.

Consoler of Erin! Are you not so?
Come in the night and the might of our woe—
In the storms that blast, and the winds that blow,
O'er our poor motherland drooping and low,
Forsaken of friend, derided by foe,
Thy mercy give, and relief bestow.
Our Lady of Knock, pray for us.

ADAPTED FROM A PRAYER PUBLISHED IN *THE WEEKLY NEWS* OF
FEBRUARY 14, 1880, AND CITED IN TOM NEARY, *I SAW OUR LADY*

Blessing

This is an ancient prayer that is said when one was going to
a healing well. Here we adapt it for our own blessing prayer.
As you say this prayer, bless yourself with holy water and/or
bless your home with holy water. Feel free to adapt this blessing to bless each room in your house by saying: "The shelter
of Mary Mother be with us in this room" (*name the room
and bless it with holy water*).

> *Holy Well,*
> *The shelter of Mary Mother*
> *Be near my hands and my feet,*
> *(Bless your hands and feet.)*

That I may go out to the well
And bring me safely home.
And bring me safely home.
(Bless your home.)
May warrior Michael aid me,
May Brigit calm and preserve me,
May sweet Brianag give me light,
And Mary pure be near me.
And Mary pure be near me.

ADAPTED FROM ALEXANDER CARMICHAEL'S
CARMINA GADELICA

Closing Prayer

Here is the earliest litany to Mary originally composed by
Brogan of Clonsast in the old Gaelic language. Respond to
each title with "Pray for us."

O Queen of Angels
O Lady of the Heavens
O Woman full and replete with the Holy Spirit
O Blessed and Most Blessed
O Mother of Eternal Glory
O Mother of Forgiveness
O Mother of the Golden Light
O Sign of Tranquillity
O Golden Casket
O Temple of the Divinity
O Fountain of the Gardens
O Washing of the Souls,
O Mother of the Orphans
O Solace of the Wretched,

O Prudent Maiden
O Cedar of Mount Lebanon
O Cypress of Mount Zion
O Purple Rose of the Land of Jacob and Rachel
O Beauty of the World,
O Ladder of Heaven.

Hear the prayer of the poor. Despise not the sobs and the sighs of the wretched. Let our groans be born by thee before the Creator for we ourselves are unworthy to be heard. O mighty Lady of Heaven and Earth, abolish our crimes and our sins, destroy our wickedness. Uplift the fallings of the feeble and the fettered. Grant to us through thee the blossoms and ornaments of the good deeds and the virtues. May we obtain through your intercession the forgiveness and pardon of all our sins and crimes. May we deserve it. May it be so. Amen.

Questions for Reflection and Discussion

1. What would be your most significant petition were you to make a pilgrimage to the shrine of Our Lady of Knock?
2. What strategies could be used to achieve in our own lives a closer reflection of God's healing love?
3. In what ways has Mary been a reflection of God's mothering love?
4. How can you be an image of a mothering God affirming your own "spiritual fecundity" and divine goodness? In what ways do you "mother" people in need of nurture and comfort?

PART III

pioneer saints of wales

Saint Non in St. Non's Chapel, Pembrokeshire, Wales. Courtesy of the authors.

CHAPTER 12

Saint Non

ICON OF HOLY BIRTHING

*Every worthwhile gift, every genuine benefit comes
from above, descending from the Creator of the
heavenly luminaries, who cannot change and is
never in shadow. God willingly gave birth to us
with a word spoken in truth, so that we may be, as
it were, the first fruits of God's creatures.*

JAMES 1:17–18 (*INCLUSIVE NEW TESTAMENT*)

Pilgrim Diary: Notes Along the Way

The ancient site of Saint Non stands high on a cliff, overlooking the sparkling waters of the Pembrokeshire coastline of Wales. Here sit the remnants of Saint Non's church which enclose the place where Saint Non is supposed to have given birth, during a violent thunderstorm, to Saint David, the patron saint of Wales. These ruins date from the Middle Ages, probably from the thirteenth or fourteenth century and are located in the midst of the standing stones from the Bronze age. According to our guide, Nonna Rees, the evidence suggests that this is an early site, since the ruins of the chapel face north and south, not east and west as was the custom in later centuries.

In a corner of the ruined walls, surrounding the field where Non gave birth to David, is a stone with a cross in the middle. On it are the marks of the hand prints of Non. This is considered the "birthing stone" of Saint Non, for, according to tradition, Non's labor pains were so agonizing that she supported herself on a stone that lay nearby and it retained the prints of her hands. Most likely, however, this stone was a sign for early pilgrims.

At the edge of the field where Non gave birth is Saint Non's well which, according to legend, sprung up as a result of the rainy deluge on the night of David's birth. This well is acclaimed for its healing power, and its waters are thought to be most potent in the cure of eye diseases. Framed by ancient stones, the well is a perfect place for reflection and prayer. Rugged stones frame the well, and primroses float in its cool waters. The day we visited, dozens of pilgrims paused at the well to pray.

In addition, up the hill near the monastery is a lovely small chapel built in 1934. Above the altar of this chapel is a beautiful stained-glass window picturing Saint Non and Saint David getting out of the boat that took them to Cornwall. Also in this chapel are stained-glass windows of the holy women Non, Winefride, and Brigit. There is a book in the back of the chapel for visitors to sign their names and make comments. Many pilgrims are touched by the peace and tranquility of this place. They leave prayer petitions on the window sills of the chapel and sign the visitors' book in the back of the chapel.

This property, on which stands Saint Non's Retreat House,

is maintained by the Passionists and Mercy sisters, Catholic religious orders that direct the center and welcome visitors with warm hospitality. It is the perfect place for a retreat or a quiet afternoon of reflection walking along the cliff top overlooking Saint Bride's Bay.

At this center we met Nonna Reese, a local expert on Saint Non, who works with individuals and groups interested in learning more about the stories of the Celtic saints in Wales. We discovered Nonna from Sister Cintra Pemberton's book *Soulfaring* published by Morehouse. Sister Cintra has led many pilgrimages to Celtic lands, and her book gives helpful resources. Although Nonna was not able to lead us on our pilgrim journey, she directed us to two splendid guides, Ann Cowie and Noragh Jones, who gave us rich background and information about the Celtic saints. Our intrepid guides even helped us journey on through a petrol strike in Wales. Though we coasted downhill a bit in our rented car, we did arrive at our departure point at Holyhead with a gallon of petrol to spare.

Encountering Saint Non

According to one *Life of Saint David*, his mother Non was a beautiful princess who was raped by a local chieftain named Sant of Ceredigion and later became pregnant and gave birth to Saint David. This *Life* expressly tells us that though Non was "outraged by violence, she otherwise continued in chastity of body and mind, and led a most faithful life."

One day, a traveling preacher named Gildas came to the Church of Ty Gwyn; and Non, who was pregnant at that time, went to hear the sermon. She stayed in the background, hiding herself in the sanctuary. Suddenly, Gildas found that he could not preach. He then asked the congregation to leave. They did; but he still could not speak. He next asked that any concealed person hiding in the sanctuary should come forth. Non came out of hiding and left the church. Gildas prophesied: "The child you are carrying will be greater than I, and the lesser cannot preach before the greater." After Non left, the congregation returned and Gildas resumed his preaching.

Legend tells us that at the time of her son's conception, two stones appeared, one at her head and one at her feet. As her delivery date approached, a local chieftain threatened to kill the child because of a the prophecies about David's greatness. This ruler, who may have been her father, began to keep watch over the place where the birth was predicted to take place.

After nine months, as Non was walking along the cliff top, near the standing stones, she went into labor. A terrifying storm arose with lightning, rain, and hail and forced Non to seek shelter. As she labored to give birth, she was surrounded by a heavenly radiance like the brilliance of the sun which protected her and calmed the elements. So terrified was the chieftain that he went away and never bothered Non again. As labor pains encompassed her, she clutched a nearby rock for support. This stone broke in half in empathy with Non as she delivered David and a spring sprang forth from the earth. According to legend, the stone became soft, and the imprint of Non's hand stayed on the stone forever.

"Whenever momentous events occur in the lives of many Celtic saints, a birth, death, or baptism," observes Nonna Rees, "the legends speak of water springing from the ground, and water is a life-force." Healing wells and healing water are recurrent themes in the Celtic sacred story. This association of water with healing dates back even to pre-Christian times. Nigel Pennick, in his book *The Celtic Saints,* makes a connection between Saint Non and an earlier goddess of similar name: "This Christian reverence of Saint Non...as mother of saints is, in some respects, a continuation of the ancient devotion to the ancestral goddess of the Celts. This mother of the gods and ancestress of the Celtic nobility was known under the names of Anna, Nonna, Dana, and other variants with the "nan" and "non" name elements....Many of the holy wells in the Celtic realms are sacred to Saint Anne and to her variants. It is probable that before the Christian religion these wells were sacred to the goddess saint."

Since the sixth century, pilgrims have walked down the steps to Saint Non's well which is about three feet deep. They would sit on a ledge in the back of the well just below the water level. Here they prayed, making an offering by dropping a coin into the well. Water carried from the well to the Saint David's Cathedral was used as a holy relic, and children were bathed in the well as a kind of baptismal ritual.

According to the custom of the Celts, Non placed David with the family of a bishop who would "foster" him, preparing him for his leadership role. In *Wisdom of the Celtic Saints*, Edward Sellner points out that the ancient Celts "developed a fosterage system in which children of one family were brought up by another family or tribe. They believed that such exchanges not only strengthened alliances but introduced each child to a wider world of learning."

It is also interesting to note that Saint Non's name means "a nun." Non responded to an invitation by her sister to be an evangelist in Cornwall. Here she established a Christian community and church at Altarnon. A stained-glass window in Saint Non's chapel depicts her journey to Cornwall. Later she went to Brittany and continued her missionary activity there. According to legend, Saint Non died in 550 and was buried in Brittany. Her tomb is said to be at Finistere. Saint Non's feast day is March 3 in Wales and is celebrated on June 25 in Cornwall.

Celebrating the Gifts of Saint Non for Our Lives

Although it is difficult to assess the personality of a person from the distant past, some conclusions can be drawn, and Nonna Rees states several: "As the daughter of a Celtic chieftain and as a princess in her own right, Saint Non would have an awareness of her own self-worth. What she leaves behind here in West Wales is a very powerful feeling of love and care. There is a softness, warmth, and a gentleness about this place. If I'm stressed out, it is here that I come. There is a strong sense of healing in this place." This feeling of love and peace is something that surely must have started here with Saint Non. Saint Julian of Norwich points to the importance of a saint being "a kind neighbor." Certainly Saint Non's spirit of kindness, of hospitality, of holy mothering is imbued in these cliffs and sea, these old stones and the timeless sky of West Wales.

Opening Prayer

O God who created us, who bore us into life,
we come before you with open hearts.
Like our Saint Non,
may we nurture life.
May we see miraculously with eyes of faith
that your providence is our Rock of Hope
in every circumstance of our lives.

*Mothering God, heal wounds that violence
   causes in our world.
Like Non, mother of Wales, may we nurture life,
   share our faith with courage, and do justice.
Amen.*

Scripture

I have looked away and kept silence,
I have said nothing, holding myself in;
But now, I cry out as a woman in labor,
gasping and panting.

ISAIAH 42:14

Reflection on Saint Non's Life

Saint Non is a reminder that all of us are birthers of the love of God. When we reach out in love to another, we are birthing God. When we serve our neighbor with warmth and compassion, even when it is not easy or convenient, when we go the extra mile for our spouse or child, when we feed the hungry and visit the sick, when we say a kind word instead of making a cutting remark, we are birthers of God's compassion. As Saint Non would admit, giving birth is painful and demanding work. So is birthing God in a world that appears caught up with consumerism and materialism.

Saint Non is also a patron of single parents and of women and men who have triumphed over abuse and violence. She is a reminder that, with God, all things are possible. There is no problem, no suffering that can come our way that God's love is not deeper still. Non provides us with a powerful model of nurturing life and faith under difficult circumstances. The legend of Non birthing David resembles a cosmic tale where the earth becomes a midwife to Non. Nature enfolds her, a heavenly radiance protects her, a rock support her. Earth and heaven hold her as she births her child. There are similarities to the birth of Jesus. Both reflect the bringing forth a royal offspring. On yet another level, this story evokes a sense that creation is partner with God in birthing new life: physical, emotional, and spiritual. In our lives, we, like Non, can be birthers of life and nurturers of faith in our relationships, in our communities, and in our work. Birthing and nurturing happens in different ways throughout our lives. It includes things like encouraging our children, planting flowers, sharing our faith, feeding the hungry in our neighborhoods and world, serving at shelters for battered women, providing foster care for children, and giving generously of our resources to support individuals and organizations who help people in crisis.

Take a few minutes to breathe deeply and slowly. Then give yourself over to the following activities.

- Imagine yourself like a child resting in God's warm embrace. Say the following prayer as a way to center: "Like a mother holding her child close to her breast, I rest in your tender embrace."
- Reflect on ways God is calling you to birth new life, nurture faith, and share with people in crisis.
- Choose a word or phrase that sums up your commitment or response to God's invitation. Write it on a rock or on some other symbol that you can use as a reminder of your commitment.
- If you are in a group, share one at a time, if you feel it is appropriate, what you have written on the rock and then place the rock in the center of your circle. As each person places a rock in the center, the group

joins hands and prays silently or aloud affirming the person's call.

Intercessions

V. For people in crisis today,

R. We lift our voices in prayer and hope to life their burden.

V. For women and men who have suffered violent abuse, and need compassion and justice,

R. We pray that they may be healed and empowered.

V. For single parents who are stressed and overworked,

R. We pray that they may guide their children to God.

V. For the lonely, depressed, and addicted,

R. We pray that they may find healing.

Follow these intercessions with spontaneous prayers, praying for any needs that are on your heart.

Closing Prayer

Saint Non, you are a patron of contemporary pilgrims who give birth to new life in a myriad of ways in our world today. In the cause of healthy opposition, your spirit lives on in women and men who oppose and overcome violence, hatred, and abuse.

Surviving the horror of rape, you clung to the rock of your faith in Christ. You remind us that no situation is so horrible that God's love cannot triumph.

Icon of a Holy Mothering, your birthing brought forth a cherished son, Saint David, patron of Wales. As a single parent, you made wise decisions in providing

for your child's care. You let God's providence be the
guide. You preached the Gospel, nurturing faith and
birthing a community in a new place.

Non, pray for single parents, who birth and nurture
their children without support in our world today.
Inspire us to give of our material and spiritual gifts,
so all will experience the support of people who care.
Amen.

Blessing Prayer

Say this simple prayer of blessing with arms extended in blessing to each person in the prayer circle.

Nurturing God,
Bless us,
Encircle us with your tender love.
In the company of Non and all Celtic holy women,
we will go forth to birth new life,
    nurture faith, and do justice
every day of our lives.
Amen.

Closing

End this ritual with the circle dance. Play Celtic music. See
Appendix 4 for directions. This dance symbolizes the inner
journey and the outer journey that we make connected with
each other and in support of each other.

Questions for Reflection and Discussion

1. What challenges do single parents face in our world to-day? How can their path be made smoother?
2. How can God's love help us not only survive but triumph over suffering in our lives?
3. Discuss women whom you admire for their triumph over violence and abuse. How are they contemporary role models for people of faith today?
4. In the process of birthing David, Saint Non left her hand prints on a stone, much like the impressions of fossils. What imprints will you leave behind for future generations?

Saint Non's Well. Courtesy of the authors.

Saint Melangell from Pennant Melangell woodcarving. Courtesy of the authors.

CHAPTER 13

Saint Melangell

PATRONESS OF ECOLOGY
AND HOLISTIC HEALING

Praise Our God from the earth,
   you sea creatures and ocean depths,
lightning and hail, snow and mist,
   and storm winds that fulfill God's word,
mountains and all hills,
   fruit trees and all cedars,
wild animals and all cattle,
   small animals and flying birds,
rulers of the earth, leaders of all nations,
   all the judges in the world,
young men and young women,
   old people and children—
let them all praise the Name of Our God.

PSALM 148:7-13 (*THE INCLUSIVE PSALMS*)

Pilgrim Diary: Notes Along the Way

An ancient pilgrimage site in the center of Wales that has reopened in recent years is Pennant Melangell. Saint Melangell's Church lies nestled in the peaceful valley of the Berwyns in Llangynog via Oswestry. The restored church is surrounded by rich flora and fauna, and there is a rushing waterfall nearby. In the circular churchyard there are some ancient yew trees which are said to be almost two thousand years old. The shrine behind the main altar in the church contains the relics of Saint Melangell, a seventh-century hermit, who founded a community in this scenic valley of the Berwyn hills.

Twelve of Melangell's nuns were buried on this site. In accordance with the Celtic custom of the time, at burial the nuns were wrapped in linen shrouds. On top of the shroud were placed white stones that indicated the number of years the religious was professed. The fact that this same tradition was observed in Iona, in southern Ireland, and in the northeast of England may indicate that it was a common practice in the early Celtic church.

The welcome brochure points out there has been a Christian Church on this site for more than twelve hundred years, and some of the present building has been here for the past eight hundred years. In the last twenty years, funding was found to restore the shrine, and by 1992 it had been reconstructed. Inside the shrine, behind the main altar, is a twelfth-century structure which is the earliest surviving Romanesque shrine in Northern Europe.

In the apse of the church is Saint Melangell's gravestone which was painted white to show that she was a religious. The grave is empty now, because the relics have been placed in the shrine. Scholars believe that in the apse floor behind the shrine are the vestiges of the ninth-century foundation which is part of the original church of Saint Melangell. Saints in ancient times were often buried in their own church.

The church also contains a fifteenth-century rood screen depicting the story of Saint Melangell. This wooden screen, which divides the eastern end of the church from the nave, also contains a rare carving of the Green Man woodland spirit prominent in pre-Christian Celtic myths.

The church is a pilgrim church and does not receive endowments or financial support from the state, but maintains itself on donations. Saint Melangell's Church is under the jurisdiction of the Diocese of Saint Asap of the Anglican Church in Wales. It is open daily throughout the year and welcomes all visitors. A certain peace permeates the atmosphere. People through the centuries have come to this steep valley surrounded by wooded slopes to find comfort, healing, and peace.

Here sheep and cattle graze on the lush grass, probably much as they did in Melangell's time. Although we did not see any wild hares running around on the day of our visit (the hare is the symbol for Melangell), there were many other wild creatures hovering in the nearby woods. On the day we visited, a cat strolled into the shrine and snuggled up on a pew near Regina, totally at home, welcoming her visitors. In ancient times, we are told, pilgrims would come into church and bring in their animals with them. Humans and animals would bed down on straw mats together.

Scholars have noted a similar pattern of friendship between humans and animals in stories of the holy ascetics in Syria, Egypt, Ireland, and Northumbria. Like the popular medieval Saint Francis of Assisi, Saint Melangell, who protected a wild hare from a hunter, could easily be called a patron saint of ecology. A Jesuit scholar, Robert Murray, is quoted in A. M. Allchin's *Journey to Pennant Melangell* as concluding that the vision of these early monastics was "to imitate on earth the ceaseless praise of the angels, and to win back the intimacy with God and the harmony with other creatures which Adam lost." Hares were often referred to in Wales as "Melangell's lambs" and have continued to be protected by the local community. Any hunter who caught a hare was expected to say "God and Melangell be with you" and release it.

A resident priest stopped to tell us the story of the foundation of this community, dating back to 607 A.D. when Melangell fled her native Ireland and settled in this valley to live a life of solitude in communion with God and with nature. According to the story, the young hermit Christianized the people of this area. Before long, a community grew up, a church was built, and Pennant Melangell became the center of a large community of nuns. Melangell's community lived a simple life close to the land. The nuns were semi-hermits, living in hovels around the church. The community used herbs and made poultices from the flora of the valley to provide healing to the local people. Local people joined the nuns for prayer, and this tradition of offering healing and reconciliation has continued through the ages. Down through the centuries, the memory of Saint Melangell was preserved in a charm often quoted by the populace: "A thousand angels and Melangell overcome the powers of evil."

A Healing Ministry of Compassionate Care

Fourteen years ago, the Reverend Evelyn Davies began her ministry of listening to people's stories of healing from cancer. This outreach has evolved into a powerful healing ministry where a group of volunteers form a community of prayer, offering healing services and intercessory prayer to thousands of people who come to Melangell's shrine from all over the world. Local hospices bring people who are near death, and many churches bring their sick here. Here in this quiet atmosphere pilgrims seek comfort from the holy Melangell, in whose presence God's healing tenderness is found. Here also a sensory garden has been created in order to combine the delight of color, smell, texture, taste, and sounds, and to be a means of comfort for those who are suffering.

Pilgrims from all over the world write out their petitions on special prayer cards and place them under Melangell's shrine. A nun from America who was blind came here for prayer. A group came from Athens and pilgrims come from all over Great Britain. Many contemplatives come here to pray. One solitary painted a lovely icon of Melangell with hare and huntsmen. There is a hidden angel on the side of a wooden carving to symbolize that we all have our hidden angels. People from all over the world phone or e-mail shrine personnel to ask that a candle be lit to remember someone who is ill or in need of special prayers. The shrine personnel send them a shrine card stating: "A lighted candle was left for you in the shrine church of Melangell today. May God and Melangell go with you." A book of intercession lists names of people for which the entire community prays.

In a small book *Journey to Pennant Melangell*, A. M. Allchin sums up the power of Melangell's legend for contemporary seekers: "The story of Melangell tells us how to the end of her days the hares were happy to run in and out among the sisters quite without fear….It is a story which speaks to us about the clash between a violent and aggressive world and a way of life which puts all its trust in God. It is a way of life which is prayerful and quiet, full of compassionate care for all living things. It makes vivid something of early Celtic Christianity which greatly fascinates people today living in a world which is very different and yet strangely similar."

Encountering Saint Melangell

Saint Melangell was an Irish princess who fled Ireland to a valley in the Berwyns in Wales to escape an undesirable marriage which her parents had planned for her. She felt called to a life of solitude and lived as a hermit in a peaceful valley for more than fifteen years. According to legend, one day, Brochwel, a local tribal chieftain, was out hunting wild animals with his dogs. Suddenly, the dogs spied a hare and chased it through the fields. The hare escaped through the thick bushes to a field where Melangell was praying and hid beneath her skirts. Soon afterwards, Brochwel arrived and ordered his dogs to capture the hare, but they refused his command. He raised his horn to signal the dogs, but his hands became paralyzed.

Stunned at Melangell's power over nature, Brochwel asked this young hermit to share her story. Melangell told the chieftain about her hermetical calling. In return for the promise of her prayers, Brochwel gave her land in the valley and declared that the valley would be a sanctuary for hares in need of protection. Thus, Melangell has been called the patron of hares.

Celebrating Saint Melangell's Gifts for Our Lives

We celebrate the memory of Saint Melangell whose hermitage and church became of place of sanctuary, not only for wild animals but for people who needed shelter and safety. Begin this ritual by practicing the breath prayers that follow.

Reciting the following prayers silently for several minutes. Soft instrumental music may be used as a background. Begin by stilling your soul and becoming conscious of God's tender love all around you.

> *Boundless Love, fill me.*
> (Breathe in deeply.)
> *Healing Presence flow through me.*
> (Breathe out completely.)

Opening Prayer

> *Author of Life,*
> *may we live in harmony,*
> *with people of every race, religion, and nation,*
> *with all creatures of the sea and on the land.*
> *May we praise you,*
> *with sun and moon,*
> *with birds and bees,*
> *with wild creatures, flowers, and trees.*
> *Like Saint Melangell,*
> *may we be quiet havens,*
> *for those in trouble.*
> *May we be precious companions on earth*
> *and kin forever in heaven. Amen.*

Scripture

"Remove the sandals from your feet, for the place on which you are standing is holy ground."

EXODUS 3:5 (NRSV)

Meditation and Reflection

Ponder the image of Melangell holding the wild hare in her arms. Spend time with this image and let it speak to you of God's gentle protection. Imagine that you are held in God's tender arms. Open your whole being to receive God's affectionate love for you. Let it flow through you and warm you, heal you, give you peace. Be aware that all beings are holy ground. You are holy ground. Repeat slowly several times, "I am holy" and "All creatures are holy." Be aware of any thoughts, feelings, or insights that emerge. Record these, if you wish, in your prayer journal.

Open yourself to receive the healing love of God in creation. Smell the flowers. Taste a raindrop. Caress the grass with your bare toes. Smile at a bug. Pet an animal. See yourself giving love to Earth, to animals and plants. See yourself as a citizen of the cosmos. Contemplate the glory of God all around you.

See yourself as a sanctuary for beings who are threatened (including wild hares). Be aware of the chaos in creation: storms, pestilence, floods, natural disasters. Is there a blessing waiting to be discovered in the devastation? Imagine yourself and all creatures held in God's embrace. Be aware of any anger or resentment you may be carrying in your heart. Breathing in, be aware of your anger. Breathing out, let it go, give it to God. Breathing in, be aware of God's compassion for the person(s) you are angry with. Breathing out, be aware of forgiveness and healing for yourself and the other(s).

Intercessions

God, our refuge,
you are a safe place for those who are threatened.
You are our anchor in chaos and confusion,
you are our comforter in loss and loneliness.
We pray for those who weep, for those who face loss,
    for those who are sick, rejected,
        and have no one to help them.
We pray for people we have been hurt by our lack of
love.
    (Pause and name them in the quiet of your heart.)
We forgive those who have hurt us.
    (Pause and name them in the quiet of your heart.)
We open our hearts to the precious earth,
    abused and polluted, and to the endangered species
        that face extinction.
We ask for healing, peace, and strength.
Let it be, let it be.

Light our path when darkness looms.
Protect us from danger and all evil.
Hold us close, forgive our failures.
Help us live together in peace and harmony with all
    creatures—great and small.
Let it be, let it be.

Add spontaneous prayers for any person or creature in
need of forgiveness, healing, refuge. Respond to each prayer
with the response, "Let it be, let it be."

Closing Prayer

> *May the love of God fill you with joy and peace.*
> *May the healing power of Christ strengthen and save*
>   *you.*
> *May the Holy Spirit encourage you.*
> *May the Spirit of Melangell surround you.*
> *May a thousand angels guide your steps.*
> *May a blessing from this holy place*
> *Protect you all your days.*

Blessing

For this blessing, walk in a circle as did the ancient Celts.

> **First Step:** *Place your arms in front of you.*
> *God be before me. You live in me and I live in you.*
>
> **Second Step:** *Place your arms behind you.*
> *God be behind me. Heal and comfort me.*
>
> **Third Step:** *Place your arms above you.*
> *God be above me. I am your marvelous creation.*
>
> **Fourth Step:** *Place your arms below you.*
> *God be below me. May I fall in love with you and*
> *with every living thing.*
>
> **Fifth Step:** *Place your arms around you.*
> *God be around me, my true home be.*

Questions for Reflection and Discussion

1. What can contemporary seekers learn from Saint Melangell?
2. How can we heal Earth? What steps can we personally take?
3. In what way(s) have you experienced the healing power of earth's creatures?
4. How can we benefit from solitude?

Saint Winefride of Holywell, Wales. Courtesy of the authors.

CHAPTER 14

Saint Winefride

RESTORED TO LIFE

One of the soldiers pierced his [Jesus'] side with a spear, and at once blood and water came out.

JOHN 19:34

Pilgrim Diary: Notes Along the Way

Our journey in search of the Celtic saints led us to Saint Winefride's shrine in Holywell, N. Wales—a place of pilgrimage since the seventh century and the only shrine in Britain that has an unbroken history of pilgrimage to the present day. Saint Winefride was beheaded by a rejected suitor and a spring flowed from the place where her head fell to the ground.

This well of Saint Winefride is located in the old town of Holywell in Flintshire. It is enclosed inside a lovely two-story Gothic building. At the bottom of the well there are some stones with red marks on them which, according to some commentators, symbolize the blood of Winefride.

The architecture of the polygonal well chamber within which the aqua waters flow is quite impressive and beautiful. The cold water that flows into this well bubbles in the center, but is peaceful at the edges. The water is channeled into a bathing area so that pilgrims can step down into the water. We did not attempt to bathe in the spring, but we did bless our bodies and drink from the well. Regina placed water on her arthritic knee and prayed for healing, while Bridget drank the holy water and prayed for a friend at home who was ill.

We met people at the well who came from as far away as India. A carving of a pilgrim carrying another pilgrim on his back is on top of the wall of the well overlooking the bathing area. There are steps on one side and others to mount on the opposite side. It was the custom to carry sick pilgrims through the water. Certainly, many pilgrims who come here carry people here in their hearts and pray for healing through the intercession of Saint Winefride.

The ritual of pilgrims walking down three steps into the water, crossing to the other side, and coming up three steps on the other side is repeated three times. Scholars believe the tradition of passing through the water three times has its origins in the Celtic rite of baptizing by triple immersion. According to the Reverend Christopher David, curate at Holywell from 1955–1964, this custom "is associated with the prayer of Saint Winefride as written down by Robert Prior of Shrewsbury in the twelfth century. This prayer requested that all who sought favors at the well "would receive an answer to their request at least at the third time." The well was almost certainly used as a baptistry in ancient times and pilgrims could profit by thinking of their penitential bathing in terms of renewing the intention and effect of baptism.

When pilgrims emerge from the cold waters, they light a candle and pray before the statue of Saint Winefride. The majestic statue depicts the princess saint with her staff in one hand and, in the other hand, a palm of martyrdom draped over her right shoulder. There is a thin line round her neck to show where her head was severed from her body and, according to the legend, miraculously restored.

The waters of Holywell has its source in the Halkyn Mountains. Originally, the waters poured into a narrow stream with sufficient power. In 1917, mining operations diverted the underground stream and the well went dry. Eventually, however, a spring of water sprung up naturally two or three hundred yards away from the same source. It was diverted and now supplies the well and valley businesses. Originally, the well produced hundreds of gallons of water a minute, but now the quantity, although plentiful, is somewhat reduced.

Time and again there were attempts to suppress pilgrimages to the shrine, but these actions only served to increase the number of visitors to the site. Many royal persons sought the intercession of Saint Winefride. King Henry V made a pilgrimage of thanksgiving from her tomb to her well in 1416. Edward IV is reported to have put some of the soil from this shrine on his crown. Richard III donated money for the upkeep of a priest at this shrine. Lady Margaret Beaufort, mother of King Henry VII, had the Holy Well parish church and chapel rebuilt in the fifteenth century. According to Francis Jones in *The Holy Wells of Wales* (Cardiff: University of Wales Press, 1954), in 1686, James II and Queen Mary of Modena visited the well "to crave the prayers of Saint Winefride that they might be blessed with a son. The King presented the chapel with part of a dress worn by Mary, Queen of Scots, at her execution and the Queen gave thirty pounds toward the fabric."

A small booklet by Christopher David entitled *Saint Winefride's Well: A History and Guide* (1964) is a wonderful source for the history and background of this sacred site.

Encountering Saint Winefride

The first printed version of the *Life of Saint Winefride* was published by William Caxton in 1485, but the legend of Saint Winefride (or Saint Gwenfrewi) has been established since the seventh century.

In the Welsh language, the name Gwenfrewi means a "radiant or holy Freda." Saint Winefride, as she is known in English, was the daughter of the local chieftain, Tewyth, and his wife, Gwenlo. Winefride was a devout child who, from an early age, felt called to devote her life to God. Her parents gave her permission to become a nun. The story is told that Prince Caradoc while out hunting one day became thirsty and dropped by Winefride's home to ask for a cup of water. From the moment Caradoc saw Winefride, he wanted to marry her. When she refused his advances, he pursued her. She fled to the church but before she could get inside, Caradoc caught up with her and in a fit of rage chopped off her head with his sword. Immediately a fountain of water sprang from the earth where her severed head lay. This is said to be the source of Winefride's holy well. Then, Saint Beuno, her uncle and priest of the church, came to the rescue, picked up Winefride's head and put it back on her body. As he prayed for her to be restored, the head and body knit together miraculously. All that remained was tiny white scar around her neck.

Beuno, in his fury, cursed Caradoc. Immediately, the earth

opened up and swallowed the lecherous nobleman. For his good deed, Beuno asked his niece for one favor—that on the feast of Saint John the Baptist a woolen cloak would be sent to him. So each year on this date, Winefride placed a woolen cloak on a stone in the middle of the river, and the stone floated down the river carrying the cloak undamaged to her uncle.

As the story goes, Winefride established a community of women in Holywell. After Beuno joined the Monastery of Clynnog Vawr, Winefride left Holywell and settled in a small double monastery of monks and nuns at Gwytherin. In time, she became the abbess of the community. She died there fifteen years after the divine intervention restored her head and was buried on All Souls' Day in the churchyard. Her relics were venerated in a wooden reliquary here until 1138 when Norman monks moved them to the Benedictine Abbey in Shrewsbury. Saint Winefride's feast day is November 3.

Elizabeth Rees in her book *Celtic Saints: Passionate Wanderers* (New York: Thames & Hudson, 2000) says that Winefride's story "is influenced by the ancient Celtic tradition that the severed head contains supernatural powers." Perhaps the more likely story is that Winefride was wounded in the throat and was nursed back to health by her mother and her uncle Bueno.

A Roman Catholic priest, the Reverend Terence Carr, who ministers at Saint Winefride's Well points out that there are few historical facts about Saint Winefride other than that she was at Holywell and later became abbess at the monastery at Gwytherin. "Places like Holywell," says Father Carr, "have a great deal to say to all generations. Holywell has been sanctified above all by a tradition of prayer which surrounds the whole shrine."

Sister Margaret Reddy, a Roman Catholic religious sister whom we met at the Pilgrim's Rest at Holywell, shared with us some stunning stories of miraculous healings that have occurred here in recent years. A woman with multiple sclerosis came to the well in a wheelchair. She did not know what prayers to say, so she said her own prayers. She had been told by a specialist that she would never walk again, but after she prayed at the well she got up out of the wheelchair and walked. In South Wales some years ago, there was a priest who had great devotion to Saint Winefride. In his parish there was a seventeen-year-old woman who was dying and who suffered with open sores on her leg. He recommended that she be taken to Saint Winefride's Well. The family brought the seriously ill woman to Holywell. For the first two days, she was too sick to go to the well. On the third day, they were able to bring her on a stretcher. As they placed her foot in the water, she saw a young girl who came up to her and placed her hand on the woman's shoulder, and told her to put her leg right down into the water. As she did so, she felt excruciating pain. But when she took her foot out of the well, her leg had a new layer of skin on it, and she was completely cured. The witnesses to this miraculous healing tried to locate the girl, but she had disappeared. People believed that it could have been Saint Winefride.

A third healing involved the family of Father Jim Collins from Liverpool. One of his brothers had a dislocated leg. He was brought to the well by his mother, and when she took the child to the doctor, he told her that she must have brought the wrong child. This boy's leg was normal.

Sister Seraphim Boyce, a hermit from Holywell who is also an artist and illustrator, shared with us the another story of a cure at Saint Winefride's Well. A married couple from China stopped at Holywell on a tour of Europe. He was an atheistic communist. His wife was a Buddhist. She had a serious problem with her wrists and had not been able to lift anything heavy. After she placed her hands in the well, she had tingling in her wrists. She told her husband that she was cured and then to the amazement of them both, she was able to lift their heavy suitcases. The following year the couple came back to Holywell to give thanks.

Sister Seraphim also told the story of Lolita who was a beautiful girl with olive skin and dark hair who suffered from hip inflammation and a fear of open spaces. Every time she had to go out, she would have panic attacks. Her husband would have to go with her. She came to Saint Winefride's Well to pray for healing. When she was standing on the third step of the well, she felt cold bubbles rising up around her hips as if the water had been boiling and frothing. But the water was fifty-three degrees. When she stepped out of the well, her pain was gone. When she went back to London, she found her panic attacks had also vanished. She went to the hospital and the doctors found no sign of hip inflammation. The doctor wrote on her medical record "cured by Saint Winefride."

Sometimes people have questions about the cures that occur at Saint Winefride's shrine. Sister Seraphim shared with us her answers to a few of the most frequently asked questions about this sacred site. Some people wonder: Does Saint Winefride heal people? Sister Seraphim's response is that God heals. Saint Winefride is an image of Christ's healing love, and she intercedes for people who pray to her. Another issue for pilgrims has to do with relics. Pilgrims come here and touch Saint Winefride's relics and are healed. So people ask, how can a relic cure people? Sister Seraphim's answer is that a relic, or a fragment of the saint's body or something that has come in contact with the saint's body is a prophetic witness to the resurrection. God is in union with the whole person, mind, body and spirit, not with just the spirit alone. As proof that a saint is with God, the Holy One remains in the saint's bones. It is as if God is saying, "I am in union with your body, mind, and heart. I will raise up your flesh up on the last day. As a proof of this union, even though your spirit is in heaven, my presence and power will remain in your bones. So it is the presence of Jesus we venerate in the relic. When you kiss the relic, it is Jesus who heals. The custom of encasing relics in beautiful jeweled containers is a reminder that God is present in the relic.

Another religious sister stationed at Saint Winefride's shrine remembers coming to the well as a sick child and being healed. Sister Laserian Fleming told about a man who came from Australia. He had promised his mother that when he had enough money he would come to the well to offer prayers in thanksgiving. Years before, when he was a baby, the doctor had told his mother to take him home and be kind to him because she would not have the little fellow much longer. His brother had taken him to Saint Winefride's Well, and now, he had been healed, he returned to give thanks for his long and healthy life.

Celebrating Saint Winefride's Gifts for Our Lives

Like Saint Non and Saint Dymphna, the story of Saint Winefride is testimony about woman-strength in the face of violence. Her story, though obviously embellished, paints a portrait of a woman who recovered after her attack and lived a meaningful life of service to God and others. Winefride was certainly the ultimate survivor—a murder victim restored to life.

Look at our society today. One step women and men can take to make a difference is by boycotting the pornography industry which exploits women and girls throughout the world. Another action we can take is to join with groups who are working to reduce the poverty that affects women and children in disproportionate numbers. We can speak up for better healthcare and education for women to prevent such crimes as female genital mutilation. We can work for stiffer prison sentences against convicted sex offenders. And, we can elect women and men of integrity to office who will draft laws that will transform our present imbalances and injustices toward women. It takes only a few people with vision and determination to change the world. Let us ask our Celtic sister, Winefride, to be our *anam chara* as we heal the wounds that damage women in our society.

Opening Prayer

This litany of Saint Winefride is excerpted from an ancient one used by pilgrims at Saint Winefride's Holywell.

> *Holy Mary, pray for us.*
> *Holy Mother of God, pray for us.*
> *Holy Virgin of Virgins, pray for us.*
> *Saint Winefride, pray for us.*
> *Glorious Virgin and Martyr, pray for us.*
> *Faithful Spouse of Christ, pray for us.*
> *Kind and Loving Virgin, pray for us.*
> *Sweet comforter of the afflicted, pray for us.*
> *Bright example of chastity, pray for us.*

Shining star, pray for us.
Fair flower of Ancient Wales, pray for us.
Chosen vessel of grace, pray for us.
Mirror of purity, pray for us.
Mirror of devotion, pray for us.
Mirror of piety, pray for us.
Shining lamp of sanctity, pray for us.
Patron Saint of Holywell, pray for us.

That we may be delivered from iniquity,
    Virgin and Martyr, pray for us.
That we may be delivered from
    disordered passions of the mind,
    Virgin and Martyr, pray for us.
That we may be delivered from deceits of the world,
    the flesh and the devil,
    Virgin and Martyr, pray for us.
That we may be delivered from occasions of sin,
    Virgin and Martyr, pray for us.
That we may be delivered from sickness,
    accident, and sudden death,
    Virgin and Martyr, pray for us.
That we may have true sorrow for our sins,
    Virgin and Martyr, pray for us.
That we may hate sin and overcome temptation,
    Virgin and Martyr, pray for us.
That we may preserve chastity and purity of life,
    Virgin and Martyr, pray for us.
That we may love humility and mildness,
    Virgin and Martyr, pray for us.
That we may persevere in prayer and penance,
    Virgin and Martyr, pray for us.

That we may bear our trials for the love of Christ,
   Virgin and Martyr, pray for us.
That those who are suffering may obtain the grace
   of patience and be comforted,
   Virgin and Martyr, pray for us.
That through thy gentle aid we may obtain health
   of mind and body,
   Virgin and Martyr, pray for us.
That Our Lady Mary may always protect us,
   Virgin and Martyr, pray for us.
That we may be worthy of the promises of Christ,
   Virgin and Martyr, pray for us.

O Blessed Winefride, pure virgin and glorious martyr, so especially chosen, so divinely graced, and so wonderfully restored from death to life. Hope of all that fly unto you with full confidence and humility. We, though unworthy, yet devoted pilgrims, make our petitions to you.

Sanctuary of piety, look upon us with patient eyes. Receive our prayers, accept our offerings, and present our supplications at the throne of mercy, that through your powerful intercessions, God may be pleased to bless our pilgrimage and grant our requests and desires, through Christ our Savior. Amen.

Meditation and Reflection

Reflect on the sparkling, clear water that sprang forth from the earth at the place where Caradoc slit Saint Winefride's throat. Here her blood mingled with the water. Pray for women and children you have known or heard about who have been abused, sexually molested, or murdered in violent circumstances. Recall the mingling of water and blood at the death of Jesus.

Reflect on your sense of self. Are there any scars, especially sexual ones, that need healing? If so, offer this area of your life to Jesus for healing. (Some deep wounds may need prayer therapy and talking therapy with a professional counselor in order to be resolved.)

Imagine yourself immersed in a fountain of God's healing love which pours like a gentle stream: soothing you, cleansing you, refreshing you, healing your wounds, giving you peace, freedom, and joy.

If you know anyone who has suffered abuse or violent attack, carry them in your heart to the Well of God's Boundless Love. Like the pilgrim Good Samaritans who carried the sick across Saint Winefride's Well, pray for this person or persons. Reflect on the healing words of Christ from Scripture, pray these words for the person or persons whom you carried to the Well of God's Boundless Love: "Let anyone who is thirsty come to me, and let the one who believes in me drink. As the scripture has said, 'Out of the believer's heart shall flow rivers of living water'" (Jn 7:37–38).

Intercessions

In this prayer, you may want to pause and name specific people you want to remember.

> *For our female ancestors, we pray for healing.*
> *For mothers and grandmothers, we pray for healing.*
> *For daughters and granddaughters, we pray for healing.*
> *For a global sisterhood in which women support other*
> *   women, we pray for guidance.*

For women who have been abused, we pray for
  empowerment.
For women who have confronted their abusers,
  we pray for your courage.
For young girls who have been sexually exploited,
  we pray for your healing.
For the support of women friends, we pray for your
  blessing.
For men who have been caring partners and
  companions, we pray for their continued growth
  and well-being.

Closing Prayer

Saint Winefride,
Be our friend and companion on our sacred journey.
With you, in the presence of God, we affirm our integrity.
Like you, our lives are holy.
May we be courageous witnesses to the Gospel of Jesus.
May we be advocates for victims of abuse and crime.
May we challenge systems that promote the
  exploitation of women.
God, let it be. God, let it be.
Amen.

Blessing

Bless to me, O God,
Each thing mine eye sees;
Bless to me, O God,
Each sound mine ear hears;
Bless to me, O God,
Each odor that goes to my nostrils;
Bless to me, O God,

Each taste that goes to my lips;
Each note that goes to my song;
Each ray that guides my way,
Each thing that I pursue,
Each lure that tempts my will,
The zeal that seeks my living soul,
The Three that seek my heart,
The zeal that seeks my living soul,
The Three that seek my heart.

ADAPTED FROM ALEXANDER CARMICHAEL'S
CARMINA GADELICA

Questions for Discussion and Reflection

1. Now focus on the scar on Saint Winefride's neck. Reflect on women today who are victims of the pornography industry. Pray for healing and justice for them. Can Winefride's story bring hope to these women? Write down any thoughts, prayers, or inspirations that you receive.

2. Decide on one thing you can do to help a woman who has suffered some form of abuse or violence in her life. Say a prayer. Write a letter. Volunteer at a shelter or crisis center. Donate resources. Boycott video, television, or entertainment networks who promote violent or pornographic materials.

3. Reflect on how you can work in solidarity with others to challenge systems that promote violence and deny human rights toward women in our society. Imagine a world in which women are treated with dignity and respect.

4. Imagine a world in which women and men are partners and equals. Write a poem or prayer, draw a symbol, sing, dance, or in some creative way, express your vision of a

Saint Winefride's Well. Courtesy of the authors.

world where women are partners and equals, treated with dignity and respect. Light a candle as a sign of your commitment to live your vision of justice and equality for women in society. Give thanks for whatever God has done for you during this time of prayer to make this dream a reality.

5. Why is Saint Winefride a role model for women in a violent society? How can faith be a resource in our response to threat and intimidation?

6. How can we, like Saint Winefride, be restored to life?

Saint Tegla in church at Llandegla, Wales. Courtesy of the authors.

CHAPTER 15

Saint Tegla

PROMOTER OF
WELLNESS AND BALANCE

*As God's chosen ones, holy and beloved, clothe
yourselves with compassion, kindness, humility,
meekness, and patience.*

COLOSSIANS 3:12

Pilgrim Diary: Notes Along the Way

We found Saint Tegla's Well near the Alun River outside of
the town of Llandegla in Clwyd with a bit of luck and our
guide's expert sense of direction. Saint Tegla's Well is the
oldest in Wales and predates the most famous Welsh Well—
that of Saint Winefride's.

If you are interested in visiting this ancient well in person,
be sure to wear boots and bring a walking stick for balance
and to get through the mud, brush, and brambles. The well
is on private land, so it is appropriate to go to Mill Farm and
ask permission to visit. Local people are helpful in giving
directions, but it is not easy to find.

These directions may assist you in finding the fifth-century well. Walk through a gate to the right of the cottages past the farm buildings. Then go over a stile by the next gate. This is a public right of way. The day we visited we had to climb over the second gate because it was locked. Then bear right and proceed across the field to a wooded area where there is a bank. If you look closely and if it is not too overgrown, you will see a sunken stone near a tree. That marks the spot where the well is located. Saint Tegla's Well was a source of fresh water during a drought in 1921 and when it was excavated in 1935, pins, coins, and other offerings were found.

While we were visiting the well, the sun broke through the trees. It felt like a heavenly presence beaming down on us. On our way back, after climbing over the locked gate, we were greeted by a cock and hens. This was appropriate due to the custom of using a rooster or hen in the healing ritual attached to this well. The local people informed us that there is a group in Llandegla interested in restoring the well. Indeed, that would be a project worth supporting and a treasure worth recovering.

The Church of Saint Tegla was rebuilt in 1866 but the old baptismal font dates to an earlier period. The church also has a beautiful brass chandelier with a crowned image of Mary, mother of Jesus, on it which probably dates back to about 1500. There is a lovely banner of Saint Tegla in the front of the church and there is information about her in the back of the church. The church is open 7:30 A.M. to 6:00 P.M. There is a wonderful bed and breakfast next to the church; its owners were was very helpful in providing information about the church and shrine.

Encountering Saint Tegla

The history of Saint Tegla seems to be intertwined with another saint named Thecla. The earlier Thecla was a disciple of Saint Paul. According to the tale, while Thecla was being thrown to the lions with other Christians, a powerful lioness came to her defense against a lion and a bear sent to devour her. In the midst of the frenzy, Thecla baptized herself. The women in the crowd threw perfumes and flowers, overwhelming the attacking beasts. The governor then released Thecla to the rejoicing of all the women. The courage and resourcefulness of Thecla became a model for Christian women in the second century.

The Welsh Saint Tegla is remembered for two miraculous cures. A man who was born blind prayed to Saint Tegla. She restored his sight by placing two bright stars in his empty sockets which immediately became a pair of new eyes. According to another story, found in Nigel Pennick's *The Celtic Saints*, Kinian, a local ruler beseeched Tegla to cure his head pain. She agreed to do so only if he set free the prisoners he had been torturing.

Which Thecla/Tegla is commemorated at this well? No one knows. We do not know the reasons the early Christian Saint Thecla and the Welsh fifth-century Saint Tegla became connected or how their stories became intertwined.

It is apparent that the story of Saint Tegla, the Celtic saint, combines both pagan and Christian elements. According to folklore, Saint Tegla's Well was associated with healing the disease of epilepsy. The ritual associated with Saint Tegla's Well combines both pagan and Christian traditions. Pilgrims would arrive at Saint Tegla's Well at sunset, a magical, liminal time. They would purify themselves by washing hands and feet in the well, walk three times around the well in a sunwise direction, chanting the Lord's Prayer while carrying a chicken. After the well-ritual was completed, they would sleep in the dark under the church altar (with the chicken) using the Bible as a pillow. When dawn came (in the old Druidic traditions dawn was another threshold time, like dusk, a magical time when healing could occur), the patient pierced the bird with pins and breathed into the hen's or cockerel's mouth. Then the patient left the chicken in the church and went back to the well. The idea was to transfer the epileptic fit to the chicken. Leaving the chicken in the church, the patient returned to Saint Tegla's Well, again walked three times around the well in a sunwise direction while reciting the Lord's Prayer three times. The seeker after healing then threw money into the well as a sacrifice of thanksgiving. Although church officials discouraged these practices, there are indications that they continued until the middle of the nineteenth century. The description of this ritual is found in a tourist booklet by Dr. Charles Kightly entitled "Enjoy Medieval Denbighshire."

Noragh Jones, our guide, believes that the spirit of Tegla still lives on this area and is memorialized in two new housing estates in the village of Llandegla named after her: "the hill of Tegla" and "the sun of Tegla."

Celebrating Saint Tegla's Gifts for Our Lives

We can learn much from the story of Tegla. One insight is that we are responsible for caring for our health. The old Celtic healing tradition focused on healing the whole person. It was not just body, but mind and spirit as well. Each of us is God's chosen. Each of us belongs to God. In our journey towards holiness and wholeness, we need to ask ourselves: are we compassionate, kind, gentle, and patient with ourselves? Do we take care of our bodies? Do we nurture our souls? Are we living a balanced and sane life? The story of Tegla's Well is a reminder of the mutuality involved in the journey to healing. There needs to be a mutuality between the person seeking healing and the person supporting the person in need of healing. We cannot simply consume healing as we consume material things. We need to enter into our own healing and channel our energies into being a whole person.

The ritual that follows can be done individually or in a group. During this prayer time, play soft Celtic instrumental music, if possible. Before beginning, place a large bowl of water on a table and a vase with water. Nearby have flowers to put in the vase during the ritual. Also have available a piece of paper and a pen.

> *Saint Tegla,*
> *Companion and Friend,*
> *journey with us to still point of our beings*
> *where we are one with God.*
> *We can't do it all or have it all.*
> *May we let go of the feverish pace that exhausts us,*
> *May we come to the Refreshing Springs of Divine Love*
> *and drink from the abundant grace*
>   *that is always there for us.*
> *Strengthen us to make the changes necessary*
>   *so we can live a more balanced, healthy,*
>   *and holy life now and in the future.*

Gather around a well, a fountain, a jar, or container of water for a contemporary adaptation of the ancient Celtic "rounds" or "patterns." Walk around the water source three times while reciting silently one word or phrase or sentence from the prayer below. It is a contemporary version of the prayer that Jesus taught us.

> *Our God, who dwells among us,*
>   *we praise your holy name.*
> *May your love be born in us.*
> *May your will be done.*
> *You give us all we need.*
> *You forgive us and help us to forgive others.*
> *You deliver us from evil and liberate us*
>   *to live in freedom.*
> *For you are the Creator, the Lover,*
>   *and the Empowerer*
>   *who enfolds us forever in your Divine Love.*
> *Amen.*

Scripture

> My child, when you are ill, do not delay,
>   but pray to the God, and God will heal you.
> Give up your faults and direct your hands rightly,
>   and cleanse your heart from all sin.

ADAPTED FROM SIRACH 38:9–10

Reflection

Close your eyes and become aware of your breathing. Become aware of your feelings. If you become aware of any worries or fears, greet the anxiety and befriend it as a loving parent who comforts a crying infant. As you breathe in and out, breathe in peace. As you breathe out, let go of your worry or anxiety.

As you breathe in, say "I am the God's beloved." As you breathe out, say "I treat myself with compassion, kindness, and gentleness." Repeat this prayer several times to relax your body, mind, and spirit.

Be aware of ways you can channel your energies into your own healing. Reflect on one thing you can do for better health and wellness. Write on a piece of paper your response to the following statement: "In order to live a more balanced and healthy life, I will commit to (*write down your response, fold the paper, and place it on the table*).

The ancient Celts had a custom of "dressing" a well by placing flowers near or in it. As soon as you are ready, go to the table, place your commitment on the tray, and put a flower in the vase.

Intercessions

V. For soundness of body, mind, and spirit, we pray.

R. May we be holy and whole.

V. That we may let go of the clutter that distracts us from living life fully,

R. May we be holy and whole.

V. For all women who work too hard and do too much, that they may find relief and relaxation, we pray,

  R. May they be holy and whole.

V. For women who feel stressed out from balancing career and home responsibilities, we pray.

R. May they be holy and whole.

V. For Saint Tegla and all healers who remind us that we can participate in our own healing.

R. May we be holy and whole.

V. For each of us and the commitments we have made to live healthy, whole, and balanced lives.

R. May we be holy and whole.

Add your own intercessions, if you wish.

Closing Prayer

> *We walk this day with God,*
> *We walk this day with Christ,*
> *The Threefold all kindly:*
> *The Threefold all-kindly.*
> *My shielding this day from ill,*
> *My shielding this night from harm,*
> *Both my soul and body...*
> *As Three and as One:*
> *As Three and as One.*

ADAPTED FROM ALEXANDER CARMICHAEL'S
CARMINA GADELICA

Blessing

> *May we be filled with peace and joy,*
> *May we live compassionately and gently,*
> *May we slow down and smell the flowers,*
> *May there be a welcome for us*
> *wherever we go,*
> *in the love of family and friends.*
> *May we our hearts be merry and rejoice!*
> *And now may God bless us and bless us kindly.*
> *Amen.*

If you wish, play lively Celtic music, participate in the Circle Dance (Appendix 4), and bless yourselves with the water.

Questions for Reflection and Discussion

1. What can we learn from the legend of Saint Tegla?
2. How can we let go of an unhealthy preoccupation that upsets the balance of our lives? How might prayer figure into the restoration of balance?
3. How can we channel our energies into the most important aspects of our lives and let go of the inconsequential?
4. Why is forgiveness important in achieving health and balance?

Modern icon of Saint Dwynwen, source unknown.

CHAPTER 16

Saint Dwynwen

PATRONESS OF LOVERS
AND RELATIONSHIPS

*"I give you a new commandment: / Love one an-
other. / And you're to love one another the way / I
have loved you. / This is how all will know that
you're my disciples: / that you love one another."*
JOHN 13:34–35 (*INCLUSIVE NEW TESTAMENT*)

Pilgrim Diary: Notes Along the Way

On a remote island off the coast of Anglesey where the Irish
sea hugs the Welsh rocks stands Saint Dwynwen's chapel
and holy well, Ffynnon Ddwynwen. Through the centuries,
pilgrims have come to this sacred site to pray for the resolu-
tion of relationship difficulties, the healing of aches and pains,
and the protection of livestock.

One ritual associated with this well was to put a handkerchief in the well; if it floated, then this was a sign that your
relationship was alive and well. If the handkerchief did not

float, this was a sign that you needed to work harder on your relationship. Another tradition, according to the Welsh poet Ceirog, is that if you bathed in the water of Dwynwen's Well, it would make you even more in love with someone than you were before.

The stories of the Celtic saints, like Melangell and Gobnait, show that their love of nature led them to choose places of great natural beauty and isolation for the establishment of their monastic foundations. Saint Dwynwen was no different. On the southwest tip of the island of Anglesey, across from what is now the little town of Newborough, amid a vast expanse of forest, sand, and rock, Dwynwen founded her retreat. So remote is this site that our guide Noragh Jones thought that locating the actual well would be almost impossible.

Encountering Saint Dwynwen

Saint Dwynwen is the patron saint of lovers, the Welsh equivalent to Saint Valentine. According to tradition, a lover who prays to Saint Dwynwen will be either healed of amorous desires or be united with the beloved. Her legend, like so many of the Celtic saints' stories, blends the magic of the ancient Druidic faith with the newly established Christian faith. Dwynwen is also associated with the goddess Venus. The "Sayings of the Wise," an old Welsh bardic collection of saintly proverbs, attributes to Dwynwen this saying: "There is none so lovable as the cheerful."

According to the Welsh story, the beautiful Dwynwen, daughter of Celtic king and Saint Brychan, falls in love with a handsome prince named Maelon. One day, he refused her love and, in a fit of anger, she spurned him. He retaliated by spreading ugly rumors about Dwynwen in their community. Dwynwen grieved deeply over her broken relationship and prayed for healing.

One night as she was sleeping, an angel appeared to her and administered a potion to her. When the angel gave the same potion to the prince Maelon, he was turned into a block of ice. After Dwynwen drank the magic potion, she was granted three wishes: (1) she asked to be healed of the pain of a broken heart; (2) she requested that her former lover would be unfrozen; and (3) she asked that all true lovers who asked for her intercession would receive help and support. All three of her wishes were granted and Dwynwen committed her life to God and founded a convent on what is now Llanddwyn Island. From that time to our present day, Dwynwen is the patron of Welsh lovers.

Noragh Jones, our guide, who shared this delightful tale with us, pointed out that in Wales people celebrate Saint Dwynwen's Day on January 25 instead of Saint Valentine's Day on February 14. They send Saint Dwywen cards to each other because she continues to be invoked by lovers and by people who suffer from unrequited love.

Celebrating the Gifts
of Saint Dwynwen for Our Lives

Modern folks can learn much from the story Saint Dwynwen. First, this story reminds us that love is mutual and that sharing love with a committed partner is a path to God. When our love is not returned, this is often a painful reality. For some, like Saint Dwynwen, it means grieving the loss, praying for healing, and offering forgiveness to the other person. Then, like Saint Dwynwen, we can use our experience to help others who suffer similar hurts and disappointments. Another insight we gain from this story is that building relationships and developing true intimacy with others requires daily acts of love in joyful times and difficult times. We need to keep renewing our commitments to keep love blossoming. In other words, love requires hard work, and the way to true love is not always a smooth one. Saints, like Dwynwen, are powerful reminders that God is love, and that even when it does not work out the way we have anticipated, love for God is our deepest calling and fulfillment.

We can grow in our ability to love and be loved by celebrating the following ritual in honor of Saint Dwynwen.

Opening Prayer

> Saint Dwynwen, your story reminds us
> that like the ocean and well waters
> mingled together in Anglesey long ago,
> we are immersed and made one in the ocean
> of your infinite and engulfing love.
> We come as we are to the wellspring of life
> with our passions and our joys,
> with our hurts and our disappointments.
> May we forgive and
> may we have the courage to ask forgiveness.
> May we encourage one another
> through good times and bad.
> May we work hard to keep our love blossoming,
> may our relationship bear fruit
> that will last forever. Amen.

Scripture

> We have come to know and to believe
>   in the love God has for us.
> God is love,
>   and those who abide in love
> abide in God,
> and God abides in them.

1 JOHN 4:16 (*INCLUSIVE NEW TESTAMENT*)

Meditation and Reflection

Use your imagination in this prayer-meditation to encircle each other with love. If possible, put on soft instrumental music in the background before you begin this reflection. Reflect on an intimate relationship or close friendship. Choose one or more of the following suggestions or let the Spirit lead you to the place where you need to be.

Open yourself to the height and depth of God's love for you and for the person you have chosen to encircle with love. Imagine yourself approaching your "beloved" and hugging him or her. Experience the Maker of Love encircling both of you in a heavenly embrace. Look into the eyes of your beloved and be still in his/her presence. Express your appreciation for the goodness you see. Share your response to one or more of the following statements with your beloved.

- I feel intimacy with you at these times.
- I ask your forgiveness for these failings.
- I forgive you for these faults.
- Together I feel we can achieve these things.
- The dream I have for our relationship looks like this.

Let your thoughts about these issues come to a natural close. Give thanks for this time together. Be aware of any feelings or insights that emerge. You may want to record these in a prayer journal or write a love letter to your beloved expressing some of your prayerful reflections.

Intercessions

V. That we may love our beloved with tenderness, we pray.
R. Those who abide in love, abide in God.

V. That we may learn to support one another, we pray.
R. Those who abide in love, abide in God.

V. That we recognize our own faults, we pray.
R. Those who abide in love, abide in God.

V. That we forgive spouses/partners/friends who have hurt us, we pray.
R. Those who abide in love, abide in God.

V. That we are grateful for each new day that we share, we pray.
R. Those who abide in love, abide in God.

V. That we let go of negativity and bitterness, we pray.
R. Those who abide in love, abide in God.

V. That we open ourselves to the mystery of our beloved, we pray.
R. Those who abide in love, abide in God.

V. That we are responsive to one another's needs, we pray.
R. Those who abide in love, abide in God.

V. That we laugh more, especially when little things go wrong, we pray.

R. Those who abide in love, abide in God.

V. That we live each day open to unexpected surprises and opportunities to grow in our relationship, we pray.

R. Those who abide in love, abide in God.

V. That we reflect divine abundance to those in need, we pray.

R. Those who abide in love, abide in God.

Closing Prayer

Saint Dwynwen, patron of lovers,
walk with us on our journey to mutual love,
deep forgiveness, and gentle healing.
May we see ourselves with the same delight
that God sees us in every moment.
May our union reflect
the passionate love of the Three-in-One,
forever loving,
forever loved.
May it be so. May it be so.
Amen.

Blessing

May the blessing of light
be on you, light without and light within.
May the blessed sunlight
shine upon you and warm your heart till it glows
like a great peat fire, so that strangers and friends
may come and warm themselves at it.
And may the light shine from the eyes of you,
like a candle set in the windows of a house,

bidding the wanderer to come in out of the storm.
And may the blessing of rain
be on you, the soft sweet rain.
May it fall upon your spirit
so that all the little flowers may spring up,
and shed their sweetness on the air.
And may the blessing of the great rains be on you,
may they beat upon your spirit
*   and wash it fair and clean,*
and leave there many a shining pool where the blue
of heaven shines, and sometimes a star.
And may the blessing of the earth
be on you, the great round earth;
may you ever have a kindly greeting
from them you pass as you're going along the roads.
May the earth be soft under you when
you rest out upon it, tired at the end of a day,
and may it rest easy over you when,
at the last, you lie out under it.
May it rest so lightly over you that
your soul may be off from under it so quickly,
and up and off, and on its way to God.
And now may God bless you and bless you kindly.
And now may God bless you and bless you kindly.
Amen.

Questions for Reflection and Discussion

1. What can we learn from the legend of Saint Dwynwen?
2. How can we let go of an unhealthy relationship?
3. How can we grow more deeply in love with our beloved?
4. Why is forgiveness important in healthy relationships?

PART IV

early
missionary
saints of
cornwall and
other celtic
saints

Stained glass triptych window behind the altar at Saint Hilda's in Upper Hutt.
Peter Janssen of Wellington.

CHAPTER 17

Saint hilda
of Whitby

MENTOR AND TEACHER

"You received freely—now freely give!"
MATTHEW 10:8 (*INCLUSIVE NEW TESTAMENT*)

Pilgrim Diary: Notes Along the Way

An epithet which might be ascribed to each of the Celtic holy women we are considering is that of "gracious giver."

In their embrace of Christianity, they were wholehearted and passionate. The "poor Christ," as Saint Ita had called Jesus, drew them with a dynamic love to aid "the least of God's children" as well as to return that love through a giving heart; and so, they gave everything away. Many of them gave away their attachment to family and home to travel as far away as the Spirit inspired them. They distributed money, food, and goods to those in need—a giving often marked more by lavish generosity than by prudence. They shared freely their education and cultural heritage with their contemporaries, their spirituality with their protegees, their living quarters with the destitute and the traveler.

Such a woman was Hilda of Whitby who is chronicled in Venerable Bede's *Ecclesiastical History of the English-Speaking People*. Bede's account is the primary source of our information about Saint Hilda. Without this account, Hilda would remain hidden in the mists of history.

We have not as yet been able to arrange a journey across England to the northeastern coast, to the town of Whitby on the Esk River to visit the cliff-top double abbey founded by Hilda. Our next pilgrimage will not ignore a visit to Hilda's Whitby, an ancient fishing port that nestles between the North York Moors and the North Sea. Since she was an advocate of Celtic spirituality, even though she was ethnically Anglo-Saxon, we cannot fail to give Hilda her due place in our chronicle of Celtic holy women. Hilda's feast day is celebrated on November 17.

Encountering Saint Hilda of Whitby

Hilda was of noble lineage. Her mother was Bregusuith, and her father, Hereric. Bede tells the story of the prediction of her birth—of her destiny to be a great light to her people. The legend goes that after her father's imprisonment by King Cerdic, who later had him poisoned, her mother dreamed that she found a strand of pearls that shone with a radiant light. Hilda would live to fulfill her mother's intuition—that her daughter was to be a pearl to her nation.

The first thirty years of Hilda's life she spent as an observant but ordinary Christian. Then, inspired by her sister, Herewith, who, after mothering Ealdwulf, king of East Anglia, had embraced a monastic life, Hilda first established a monastery north of the Wear River under the guidance of Bishop Aidan. Later she became Abbess of Heruteu (Hartlepool). Here she gave organization to the monastic life by establishing a "rule of life." Her rule saw to it that no one lived richly, but that each member shared the common life.

Her double monastery at Whitby, where monks and nuns alike contributed to the common monastic life, was also an educational center which schooled several boys who became bishops. Bede tells how Hilda fostered the talent for poetry of one of her lay brothers, Caedmon. With her encouragement, what is known as "Caedmon's Hymn" became the first lyric poem in Anglo-Saxon; and the monk continued to create other religious lyrical poetry.

As abbess of Whitby, she hosted King Oswy's Council of Whitby, at which, in 664, the style of spirituality and religious practice for the whole of Northumbria was decided. Following the example of Paulinus and Aidan, Hilda favored the Celtic model of church over the Roman. The Celtic observance differed from the Roman in style of tonsure, in the dating of Easter, and in Church organization as monastic, under an abbot or abbess, rather than diocesan—under a bishop. Ultimately Oswy decided in favor of Roman practice for his kingdom. Choosing this course meant that all of England would be held to the same observances. Though Hilda supported Oswy's decision, she continued the Celtic tradition throughout her life.

Bede states that her followers called her "mother" and that this designation singled her out as a wise spiritual guide. Indeed, she served as an *anam chara* for both wealthy and poor who sought her counsel. Bede refers to her as a leader in pursuing peace, justice, and love.

In her later years, Hilda suffered a long, six-year illness with periodic high fevers; but she continued in her monastic duties and leadership, until, during a final bout with an infection, she died on November 17 in 680 A.D. at the age of sixty-six, counseling her people to preserve their blessed "evangelical peace among themselves and with all others."

Bede narrates the story of a vision, seen by one of Hilda's novices at the time of her death. The young woman told her fellow sisters that she had seen Hilda's soul ascending to heaven surrounded by angels. Is this simply a literary convention appended to Hilda's story by Bede in order to emphasize her holiness? Or is it a recounting of an actual, reported incident by one of her nuns? Who can say? Only a few months ago a friend recounted attending the funeral of a man everyone revered as holy, and of seeing, on the wall of the chapel, an ascending light. Several people noticed the phenomenon, coupled with a peaceful inner experience that the deceased was in God's presence.

A similar story is part of the oral tradition of the Webster side of Regina's family. The Websters owned mountainous farmland in Virginia's southwest Blue Ridge area. Among family lore is the tale of a fragile little boy named "Benny" whom everyone loved because of his gentle ways. One winter when Benny was about seven, his weakened lungs didn't make it through the bleak weather, and in February Benny died. There was much grief in the extended family of aunts, uncles, and cousins, as well as in his immediate family; until, during the wake, people noticed the figure of a small child in the distance—a shadow, really, in the dim twilight—carrying a lantern as he made his way slowly up the mountainside. The phenomenon was witnessed on successive nights; and everyone concurred that little Benny was on his way to God.

Celebrating Saint Hilda of Whitby's Gifts for Our Lives

What is Saint Hilda's legacy to us? As one of the major figures of the seventh century, she exemplifies a model of mentoring as shown by her encouragement of the uneducated herdsman Caedmon, who is known as the first English poet. It is seen in her love of Scriptures which she nurtured among the monks and nuns of her monastery. We can emulate also her desire to live in harmony with others as shown by her deathbed advice and her willingness to compromise and share. And we can benefit from modeling ourselves after Hilda's common sense and good judgment. We need to contemplate these characteristics as we celebrate Hilda's gifts to us.

Opening Prayer

God of beauty and author of all creation,
your friend, Hilda, was a leader you could trust
to foster in others their giftedness.
Make me an "enabler," a fosterer the gifts of others.
May I not let jealousy or a competitive spirit
    prevent me
from affirming the goodness of those around me.
And, beyond the nurturing of others,
help me to find real joy in their blessings.
I ask this of you and give praise to you,
who are the Source of every good gift.
Amen.

Scripture

"If you bring your gift to the altar and there remember that your sister or brother has a grudge against you, leave your gift there at the altar. Go to be reconciled to them, and then come and offer your gift."

MATTHEW 5:23 (INCLUSIVE NEW TESTAMENT)

Reflection

Begin this time of prayer by quieting your mind and body. Become completely still. Open yourself to the Gracious Giver dwelling within you.

Reflect on the ability Saint Hilda possessed to affirm others in their giftedness and, thus, to foster their growth. There are opportunities in your life to nurture the giftedness of others. Think of times when you have done so. Reflect on times when you might have done so, but did not. Ask yourself how has God's love flowed through this person to you. Give thanks for each gift or quality that you discovered. You may choose to record your responses in a prayer journal.

Be attentive to the ways God is working your life. Give thanks for the gifts God has given you to love and nurture others. You may choose to record your responses in a prayer journal.

Pray the paraphrase of the hymn of Caedmon below. Let these praises fill you and, then, add to them your own praises.

> *Praise the Creator of Heaven.*
> *How good of the gracious God*
> *to fashion for us a heaven of joy!*
> *Praise Your power, wonderful Creator,*
> *and Your Wisdom made known to us,*

even to us simple ones,
the products of your creative will.

I praise your deeds, Glorious One, our eternal God!
For You authored all the marvels that exist around us.
And then, for our benefit,
  you made the heavens as our roof,
And the solid earth as our footrest.
Praise be! Praise be!

Intercessions

V. For a grateful heart, we pray.

R. Gracious Giver, open us to your love.

V. For the ability to affirm others' gifts, we pray.

R. Gracious Giver, open us to your love.

V. For eyes to see the marvels of creation around us, we pray.

R. Gracious Giver, open us to your love.

V. For a generous spirit to serve others, we pray.

R. Gracious Giver, open us to your love.

V. For the wisdom to use our own special gifts, we pray.

R. Gracious Giver, open us to your love.

V. For blessings on those who struggle with negative attitudes toward self and others, we pray.

R. Gracious Giver, open us to your love.

V. For teachers, that they may encourage students to excel, we pray.

R. Gracious Giver, open us to your love.

Closing Payer

Generous God, thank you for people
who have affirmed our goodness.
Like Saint Hilda, may they become like bright stars
shining in the heavens
for we have walked in their glorious light.
Like Saint Hilda, may we become "gift givers,"
generous reflections of You,
the Gracious Giver in our midst.
Glory and Praise to You, now and forever.
Amen.

Blessing

I am lying down tonight with God,
and God tonight will lie down with me.
I am lying down tonight with the Holy Spirit,
and the Holy Spirit this night will lie down with me.
I will lie down this night with the Three of my love,
and the Three of my love will lie down with me.

ADAPTED FROM ALEXANDER CARMICHAEL'S
CARMINA GADELICA

Questions for Reflection or Discussion

1. Have you reflected recently on your own gifts? What are they? Make a list of them. Thank God for them.
2. Sit in a circle with others who are sharing these thoughts. On a piece of paper, write the name of the person on your right. (Everyone in the circle should do the same.) Now, write one gift which that person possesses which you appreciate. Pass the paper to the person on your left.

Read the name at the top of the paper you have just been handed. Write one gift which that person possesses which you recognize. Continue this process until each person receives the paper with his/her name at the top.

Read over the comments others have made about your gifts. Did you know these were true of you? Are you somewhat surprised?

Here is one last step, if you are up to it. Each person may read aloud the list of the gifts the group has affirmed of him or her. In a group prayer, thank God who is the Gift-giver!

3. In what ways do others need our gifts today?
4. How can we be gift-givers to people in need in our world?

Traditional Celtic knotwork design, 7th century

CHAPTER 18

Saint Ía

MISSIONARY TO CORNWALL AND BEARER OF GOD NEWS

Jesus came forward and addressed them in these words:

> *"All authority has been given me*
> *both in heaven and on earth;*
> *go, therefore, and make disciples of all the nations.*
> *Baptize them in the name*
> *of Abba God,*
> *and of the Only Begotten,*
> *and of the Holy Spirit.*
> *Teach them to carry out*
> *everything I have commanded you.*
> *And know that I am with you always,*
> *even until the end of the world!"*
>
> MATTHEW 28:18—20 (*INCLUSIVE NEW TESTAMENT*)

Pilgrim Diary: Notes Along the Way

Numerous Celtic missionaries found their way to Cornwall, carrying the good news of Christ Jesus as savior and redeemer. Many of these missionaries were women who took the Gospel admonition to go into the whole world and spread the "good news," equally seriously for their lives as did their male counterparts. In their zeal they thought nothing of taking risks; and of those who went to evangelize Cornwall, many were martyred. Little is known about most of them; but in Cornwall there are still some vestiges of their influence in place names and holy wells.

Peter Berresford Ellis in his *Celtic Women: Women in Celtic Society and Literature* mentions that among the twenty missionaries to Cornwall were the "nine daughters of Brychan, a sixth-century king of Powys in Wales, Adwen (Dwynwen in Wales) who became the patron saint of Cornish sweethearts, Endelienta, Juliot, Keria, Keyne the beautiful, Mabyn. Minver, Teath and Wenna." A list of other women missionaries includes Crida, Ewe, Gulval (Wovela), Merteniana, and Sitofolla, sister of Paul Aurelian, a Celtic saint whose *Life*, written before 1000 A.D., still exists. After establishing monasteries in Sidwell and Laneast, Launceston, Sitofolla settled in Saint Mount's Bay in Cornwall.

Piala and her brother, Gwinear, fifth-century missionaries, landed in the Hayle estuary in Cornwall, but their mission was short-lived, because the ruler of the region, Tewdrig, promptly executed them. Other fifth-century female missionaries to Cornwall were Breaca, Crowan, Buryan—daughter of a Münster chieftain—for whom a village is named, and Ia, also a chieftain's daughter, whose name is reflected in the town of Saint Ives.

The holy well of Saint Ia is located by the side of Porthmeor Hill, below the graveyard overlooking Porthmeor Beach. It consists of two rectangular recesses in a granite wall, each containing a supply of water. On top of these granite walls is a plaque stating the well was used as a main water supply for the old part of Saint Ives until 1843. Though we have yet to make the trek to Saint Ia's Well in West Penwith, Cornwall, this site is on our agenda for our next journey.

Encountering Saint Ia

Ia's legend has a special appeal. Seemingly she was petite, and perhaps, fragile. For some reason her traveling companions, men and women, left before her arrival at the Irish port. Either, as some accounts suggest, they considered her too frail for the journey or, as others say, she arrived late at the place of embarkment. Whatever the reason, Ia grieved deeply to have missed her missionary opportunity, so strong was her desire to evangelize.

Disappointed, Ia stood at the water's edge, staring at the spot where the boat, long since embarked, had been moored. Floating on the tide, she saw a leaf. "Oh, that you might carry me to the land where my companions have gone!" She spoke to the leaf; and touched it with her walking staff. Miraculously, it grew, so goes the legend, into a coracle large enough to support her. In she climbed, and the amazing boat carried her swiftly to Cornwall to the area now named for her.

There she managed to live in harmony with her neighbors and to convert them to Christianity; whereas those who were originally to have been her companions, Fingar, Kew, Buryan, Pialla, and Ia's two brothers, landed in a different place and some of them, at least, were martyred shortly after their arrival.

There is an ancient style of Irish boat, a coracle, which is somewhat leaf-shaped; and one source suggests that its leaf-like appearance may in part account for the legend of Saint Ia.

The chief of the area now called Saint Ives was evidently impressed with Ia, because he built her a church. The parish of Saint Ives near the harbor has a stone baptismal font which dates from medieval times, and a beautiful lady chapel with paintings, and woodcarvings of the Celtic saint. Saint Ia's tomb is also there. Saint Ia's story is told in the *Life of Saint Gwinear* by Anselm, a Breton cleric, who wrote around 1300 A.D.

Saint Ia's feast day is celebrated on February 3, and the following Sunday a special Mass and procession are held in her honor. The whole town celebrates a public holiday of "Feast Monday," during which a ball made of cork and encased in silver is used in a kind of early football.

Celebrating Saint Ia's Gifts to Our Lives

What can Saint Ia teach us today? Certainly her faith in crossing the sea on a leaf seems firmer than the faith of Saint Peter trying to walk on water. We can also learn that missing the boat may not be that bad occurrence it is reputed to be. In the following prayer-ritual, let us celebrate the persistent faith of Saint Ia, evangelist from Ireland.

Opening Prayer

> *O God of Stormy Waters,*
> *so frail is our boat, so powerful the sea,*
> *lead us and we will follow you,*
> *set us freely afloat even in the midst of our fears.*

May your Presence come between us and all things evil.
May we believe that all things are possible with you,
that no threat will overwhelm us,
for Everlasting is your love.
Open before us your vision for our world,
So we may see your glory in our midst.
We consecrate ourselves to your service this day.
Amen.

Scripture

Jesus insisted that the disciples get into the boat and precede him to the other side. Having sent the crowds away, he went up on the mountain by himself to pray, remaining there alone as night fell. Meanwhile the boat, already a thousand yards from shore, was being tossed about in the waves which had been raised by the fierce winds.

At about three in the morning, Jesus came walking toward them on the lake. When the disciples saw Jesus walking on the water, they were terrified. "It is a ghost!" they said, and in their fear they began to cry out.

Jesus hastened to reassure them: "Don't worry, it's me! Don't be afraid!"

Peter spoke up and said, "If it is really you, tell me to come to you across the water."

"Come!" Jesus said.

So Peter got out of the boat and began to walk on the water toward Jesus. But when he saw how strong the wind was, he became frightened. He began to sink, and cried out, "Save me!"

Jesus immediately stretched out his hand and caught Peter. "You have so little faith!" Jesus said to him.

MATTHEW 14:22–31 (*INCLUSIVE NEW TESTAMENT*)

Meditation and Reflection

Pray a prayer asking for Ia's courage—the bravery of a zealous heart:

> *I hear your words, Jesus:*
> *"Go and teach all nations…."*
> *Each of us has our own call.*
> *I believe I am now at a place*
> *where you wish me to be.*
> *Where you may wish me to go next,*
> *I do not know;*
> *but I wish to be ready and willing*
> *to go wherever my life leads me,*
> *for then I shall be where You have called me to be.*
> *I believe that my desire to serve you, does,*
>   *indeed, please you.*
> *Show me how I may spread the "Good News"*
>   *of your Coming*
> *among us right where I find myself in life now.*
> *Show me how I may share my faith with others,*
> *and fulfill your injunction.*
> *Let me be, like Ia, full of zeal!*
> *Let me believe that You are, in fact, leading me.*
> *I am not alone. You are with me.*

In the legend, Ia was somewhat small and fragile—not the kind of person one would think capable of taking on a difficult journey and challenging task. But, her love for God was a consuming blaze which filled her with daring. She didn't seem even to notice her limitations.

Sometimes we put limitations on ourselves; thinking we

are too incapable to do this, or not talented enough to do that. Perhaps we need the fire of the Holy Spirit to move us beyond our limiting mind-set. With ardent desire, then, pray the traditional prayer asking the Holy Spirit for that zeal:

> *Come, O Holy Spirit,*
> *Fill my heart.*
> *I want to be Your faithful one.*
> *Enkindle in me the fire of your divine Love.*
> *O God, send forth your Holy Spirit to fill me,*
> *And I shall be re-created in You;*
> *That You may renew the face of the earth.*

Now make for yourself a mantra, or chose one of the following, and repeat it for several minutes.

- *Kindle in me the fire of Your Divine Love.*
- *God, bless my body and soul, they are yours.*
- *God, I trust that you are with me always.*
- *God loves through me.*
- *God has no hands, but my hands.*
- *God has no feet, but my feet.*
- *Today, God has come.*
- *I am in God.*
- *God dwells in me.*

The legend of Ia tells of miraculous happenings, but it also tells of ordinary successes–for example, that of the king of the area of Cornwall being impressed enough by Ia to support her as foundress of a Christian settlement, and to build her a church. In our own lives, there are things that happen that sometimes seem to border on the miraculous. There are also wonderful things which would not be called "miracles," but which clearly speak to us of God's providence and protection. Look back over your life to discover some of these. Thank God for being with you. Share these miracles with others.

Intercessions

V. For people who suffer from stress and loneliness, we pray.
R. God, let me see you in others.

V. For people who need a helping hand, we pray.
R. God, let me see you in others.

V. For strangers who have no one to welcome them, we pray.
R. God, let me see you in others.

V. For people who are homeless, we pray.
R. God, let me see you in others.

V. For people who suffer from addictions, we pray.
R. God, let me see you in others.

V. For people who are physically or mentally challenged, we pray.
R. God, let me see you in others.

V. For people who feel depressed, we pray.
R. God, let me see you in others.

V. For people who have lost their way, we pray.
R. God, let me see you in others.

V. For people who need my/our help today, we pray.
R. God, let me see you in others.

Closing Prayer

Christ with me.
Christ before me.
Christ behind me.
Christ in me.
Christ beneath me.
Christ above me.
Christ on my right.
Christ on my left.
Christ when I lie down.
Christ when I sit down.
Christ when I arise.
Christ in the heart of everyone who thinks of me.
Christ in the mouth of everyone who speaks of me.
Christ in the eye of everyone that sees me.
Christ in the ear of everyone that hears me.
Christ ever be.

PRAYER OF SAINT PATRICK

Blessing

Be each saint in heaven,
Each sainted woman in heaven,
Each angel in heaven,
Stretching the way for you,
When you go thither
   Over the river hard to see;
Oh, when you go thither home
   Over the river hard to see.

ADAPTED FROM ALEXANDER CARMICHAEL'S
CARMINA GADELICA

Questions for Discussion and Reflection

1. What does the large number of Celtic missionaries back in the fifth and sixth centuries tell us about the quality of their faith and the depth of their love of Jesus? Are there people today who do such things?

2. Are there ways in which those of us who are not called to foreign lands but are destined to remain near our families are called to be bearers of the good news of Jesus?

3. What kind of prayer life must one have to gain the kind of courage it takes to live the ideals of Jesus in today's world? How deeply in love with Jesus must one be to take on the demands of living fully the Christian life?

4. When a Kerry woman was asked where heaven was, she answered, "About a foot and a half above you." How can we find the glory of God in our midst?

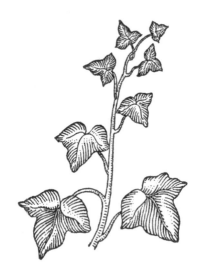

CHAPTER 19

Other Saints
Of the
Celtic Tradition

The following brief portraits provide glimpses of Celtic Holy Women we discovered in our research, but whose sites we did not visit with the exception of Saint Innywee.

Saint Innywee: Healer of Warts

 In County Clare, Ireland, in "the Burren," six-tenths mile beyond the Poulnabrone Dolmen, is a well sacred to Saint Innywee. Innywee is an anglicized spelling for "Inghean Bhaoith," which translates "daughter of Baoth." Her feast day has been celebrated in County Clare on December 29 for many centuries. Inghean Bhaoith's monastery was at Killinaboy (the church of the daughter of Baoth). Over one of the doorways is a *sheela-na-gig*, known as Baoith, named after the cow-Goddess Boand. Once again, the interweaving of the pagan and Christian attributes of goddess and saint is evident.

The well of Innywee is just outside the wall of Paddy

Healy's farm—the first turn to the left, marked "the cottage" on the road to Ballyvaughan from Corofen. As Paddy Healy tells it: "When I was young a lot of people, mainly people from around here, would come to this well for a cure for warts. A bit out from the well there is a mound, and there people would come to 'make the rounds'—to pray Our Father's, Hail Mary's, and Glory Be's as they walked around the well. They would make the rounds on three days: Tuesday, Thursday, and Sunday, and they always left some little thing: a medal, a coin, or ribbon tied to a nearby tree—something to mark their visit." (This information is from an interview with Paddy Healy and from a booklet by George Cunningham entitled "Burren Journey," published by the Midwestern Regional Tourism Organization, 1978.)

Saint Gwen Teirbron: Patroness of Nursing Mothers

 In ancient times, nursing mothers would pray to Saint Gwen that through her intercession they would have an ample supply of breast milk to feed their babies. Images of Saint Gwen which show her with three breasts indicate that Gwen, like the earlier precursors, had an abundant supply of breast milk to nourish her children. In Britain, Saint Gwen was known as Saint White or Saint Wita or Saint Candida. In Brittany, this nursing mother saint was also well known. Nigel Pennick recounts this information in his book *The Celtic Saints* (New York: Sterling Publishing Company, 1997).

Saint Helen Luyddog: Patroness of Travelers

Saint Helen Luyddog is sometimes confused with Saint Helena, the mother of Constantine. "Although little is known about her historically, Nigel Pennick, observes that many roads across Wales, called Sarn Helen, Ffordd Elen and Llwybr Elen, bear her name…. There are also a number of holy wells in Wales named after her."

Saint Tannoch: Patroness of Survivors of Violent Crimes

Tannoch was the Christian daughter of Loth, a pagan chieftain. Loth wanted his daughter to marry Prince Ewan, but Tannoch had already made up her mind to dedicate her life to service of God. So, her father threw her out of the family home. Tannoch found a safe refuge with a swineherd and his friends. One day her peaceful world was shattered when Ewan found her alone and raped her. Tannoch became pregnant. Furious at his daughter's disgrace, Loth had his daughter thrown down Dunpelder, a seven-hundred-foot drop on the south side of Traprain Law. As she fell, Tannoch cried out to the Blessed Mother for help. When her friends found her at the bottom of the precipice, they were amazed. Tannoch was not injured. But this did not dissuade her father from further action against his daughter. This time he put Tannoch in a coracle (a small boat) near the Isle of May. The rough sea and wind carried her up the coast to Culross where she gave birth to a son. Here she was befriended by shepherds who brought her to Saint Serf. An ancient manuscript describes the joyous occasion: "The blessed old man was filled with spiritual laughter and his heart with joy at the sight of the baby." Saint Serf name the baby Kentigern, also known by the nickname "Mungo," which means "my dear friend." Kertigern later became a bishop who was known for his life of prayer and simplicity. This information is derived from Courtney Davis and Elaine Gill's *The Book of the Celtic Saints* (London: Blandford, 1995).

Saint Tydfil : A Herbal Healer

 Saint Tydfil was the daughter of Irish parents who moved to Brecknockshire in Wales. One of several siblings born to Brychan and his wife, she is said to have been an artist of the wild life that surrounded her in the beautiful Welsh countryside. She is also credited with a knowledge of the healing properties of herbs.

Eventually she became a hermit in the area known as "Merthyr Tydfil" (translated: "the martyr Tydfil") where she used her herbal remedies for the local people who attributed many cures to her skill. On a trip to visit her ailing father she was killed by outlaws, and hence came about the name of the area where she had resided as a prayerful recluse: "Merthyr Tydfil." Her feast is celebrated on August 23. This Celtic holy woman is mentioned in Johanna O'Mahony Walters's *Tales of Travel and Trust: Our Celtic Heritage* (Dublin: Veritas, 1999).

Saint Caitigern: Monastic Founder

 Jack Roberts in his *Sacred Mythological Centers of Ireland* (Bandia, Ireland) tells us of Saint Caitigern who founded Kilcatherine, an early Christian monastic settlement near Eyeries overlooking Coulagh Bay on the Beara peninsula in southwest Cork, Ireland. There is a stone head on the entrance into the ruins which scholars think is a cat-like image. One of the earliest ancient Christian crosses still stands in the churchyard. According to legend, Saint Caitigern turned the Cailleach or Hag of Beara, one of the most powerful goddesses of the pre-Christian world, into stone. The word "Cailleach" or Hag means a wise, spiritual woman. The rock which is associated with the Hag of Beara is located less than a mile from Kilcatherine.

Annotated
Bibliography

Adam, David. *Border Lands: The Best of David Adam's Celtic Vision*. (Franklin, Wis.: Sheed & Ward, 1991.) The prayers and invocations in this book draw us into the depths of the ancient Celtic soul and open us to a new insight into this powerful mystic tradition. One example: "*O Being of Life! O Being of peace! O being of time, and time without cease! O Being, infinite, eternity!*"

Allchin, A. M. *Journey to Pennant Melangell: A Welcome for Pilgrims*. (North Powys, Mid-Wales, 1997.) This booklet was written to provide a brief reflection on the history of Pennant Melangell and the meaning of the life and witness of Saint Melangell.

Allchin, A. M. *Pennant Melangell: Place of Pilgrimage*. (Oswestry, Wales: Gwasg Santes Melangell, 1994.) This booklet gives a wonderful introduction to Pennant Melangell, the coming of the saint, the history of the shrine, and quotes poems written in honor of Melangell. It describes the feeling of peace and presence pilgrims experience when they come to this magnificent valley with its wooded slopes, grazing sheep, and serene atmosphere.

Buckley, Maria. *Celtic Spirituality*. (Cork: Mercier Press, 2001.) This resource provides a comprehensive overview of Celtic spirituality and its antique roots in the druidic culture of the past in a language and style easy to understand. The transition from a Celtic, monastic, uncentralized religious practice and spirituality to a highly controlled, organized and authoritarian model as Roman practice overshadowed Ireland's more indigenous traditions is explained.

Cahill, Thomas. *How the Irish Saved Civilization: The Untold Story of Ireland's Heroic Role from the Fall of Rome to the Rise of Medieval Europe.* (New York: Doubleday, 1995.) This book is a scholarly but enjoyable overview of Celtic history. Cahill's presentation of the role of abbesses "whose hands had the power to heal, who almost certainly heard confessions, probably ordained clergy and may even have celebrated Mass" is a claim worthy of further investigation.

Caldecott, Moyra. *Women in Celtic Myth: Tales of Extraordinary Women From the Ancient Celtic Tradition.* (Rochester, Vt.: Destiny Books, 1988.) In this book, we meet Celtic heroines such as Macha, Arianrod, the Morrigu, and Maeve. These powerful stories lead us a deep recognition of female strength and help us to make a universal connection with the mystery of being at the heart of existence.

Carmichael, Alexander. *Carmina Gadelica: Hymns & Incantations, Collected in the Highlands of Scotland in the Last Century.* (Edinburgh: Floris Books, 1992.) Alexander Carmichael (1832–1912) traveled the Highlands and Islands to gather the oral poetry and song of the people. This venture resulted in this extraordinary collection of hymns, prayers, charms, rituals, and incantations. No one knows who composed the Gaelic originals, they were handed down through generations by oral tradition. This book is a great treasure.

Carroll, Michael J. *A Bay of Destiny: A History of Bantry Bay and Bantry.* (Dublin: Color Books, 1996.) Michael Carroll provides a comprehensive overview of Irish history of this area from about 1500 B.C. to the present. He includes interesting insights into the Brehon Law and to Saint Cannera's (Caner's) foundations and a holy well.

Carthy, John. "*Patrican Beginnings*," *Holy Trinity Church Ballinalee Rededication, June 18, 1995.* (County Longford, Ireland: Rapid Print Ltd., 1995.) [Material provided by John and Patricia O' Reilly who currently reside on property which was part of the ancient monastic site of Saint Samthann's foundation in Old Clonbroney, Co. Longford.] This booklet provided some interesting information linking Saint Patrick to Clonbroney. According to tradition, Patrick installed his two foster sisters, the two Emers, as heads of a community of women in Clonbroney, which some claim as the first nunnery in Ireland. "Clonbroney" translates "the field of Bronaighe" who was an early abbess of the monastery. To this day there are people in Clonbroney who bear the name: "Emer" and "Bronach." The local school has had two names. In 1949 it was called "*Scoil Bronaige,*" but was later changed to "*Scoil Samthann*" who was abbess from 728 to 734 A.D.

Clancy, Padraigin. *Celtic Thread: Exploring the Wisdom of Our Heritage.* (Dublin: Veritas Publications, 1999.) This outstanding book is a collection of essays which raise important questions about the legacy of the ancient Celtic tradition on contemporary spirituality. It features contributions from prominent Irish women and men well worth reading, including Mary Condren "The Uncreated Conscience of Our Race"; Dolores Whelan, "Celtic Spirituality: A Holy Embrace of Spirit and Nature"; Mary Minehan "Kildare Today: Continuing the Brigidine Tradition." In her essay, "Brigit: Muire Na nGael (Mary of the Gael)," editor Padraigin Clancy's stresses that the stories of the ancient female saints need to be told and retold because they are not well known and because these women represent the eternal feminine in the Celtic tradition. This is precisely the reason for the creation of this book.

Connolly, Susan, and Moroney, Anne-Marie. *Stone and Tree Sheltering Water: An Exploration of Sacred and Secular Wells in County Louth.* (Drogheda, Ireland: Flax Mill Publications, 1998.) The authors visited about a hundred wells in County Louth, Ireland. In this book they wrote about the healing attributes of the wells, location, accessibility and quality of water.

Their directions for finding these wells are excellent. Their recommendation to wear warm clothes, wellington boots, bring a walking stick, a flashlight, and a cup is wise advice!

Condren, Mary. *The Serpent and the Goddess: Women, Religion and Power in Celtic Ireland.* (San Francisco: Harper and Row, 1989.) A study of the treatment of women in myth, church, history, and politics in Ireland. The study ranges from pre-Christian, early Christian, and late medieval Ireland, and explores the contemporary consequences of decisions taken and political structures established during those eras. Mary Condren's analysis of Brigit of Kildare is a highlight of the book. This is a must-read scholarly work for a serious student of the feminine face of the Celtic Ireland from a prominent, contemporary Irish feminist theologian.

Condren, Mary. *"Brigit: Soulsmith for the New Millennium,"* ed. Elizabeth Schussler Fiorenza in CONCILIUM (Dec 2000). New insights into Saint Brigit are presented.

Condren, Mary. *"Gender and Representation"* and *"Celtic Spirituality"* entries in Dictionary *of Feminist Theologies*, eds. Letty Russell and Shannon Clarkson. (Louisville, Ken.: Westminster, 1996.) The author provides fresh insights into the use of gender-specific terminology in relation to the Celtic world-view.

Cronin, Deborah K. *Holy Ground: Celtic Christian Spirituality.* (Nashville: Upper Room Books, 1999.) The author looks at aspects of Celtic Christianity and reflectively applies them to her own life-experiences.

Dames, Michael. *Mythic Ireland.* (London: Thames and Hudson, 1992.) This is an in-depth study of the Celtic myths which provided a kind of "old testament" for the coming of Christianity. The author discusses each of the five kingdoms: Ulster, Münster, Leinster, Connacht, and the "middle kingdom" of Mide in connection with its particular regional myths. This has been republished in larger print with color pictorial additions under the title: *Ireland, A Sacred Journey.* (Shaftesbury, Dorset: Element Books Ltd.), 2000.

David, Reverend Christopher. *Saint Winefride's Well: A History & Guide.* (Holywell, North Wales, 1971.) This booklet provides a comprehensive history of Saint Winefride's Well. It features helpful black-and-white photographs of carvings in the shrine and the perpendicular architecture of the well chapel. Letters from medieval times are cited, describing Saint Winefride's Well as a place of pilgrimage since the seventh century for kings, queens, and people alike. This illustrated description proudly asserts that Saint Winefride's is "the only shrine in Britain that can show an unbroken history of pilgrimage to the present day."

Davies, Oliver. *Celtic Spirituality*. (Mahwah, N.J.: Paulist Press, 1999.) This is a scholarly collection of texts translated from Irish, Welsh, and Latin. A basic theological premise of Celtic Christianity is summed up: divine Presence and power flows through Mary, the angels, and the saints. This book features two important lives of Brigit. The story of Brigit's ordination by Bishop Mel in all its delightful detail is contained in *The Irish Life of Brigit*.

Davies, Oliver, and Bowie, Finoh. *Celtic Christian Spirituality: An Anthology of Medieval and Modern Sources*. (New York: Continuum Publishing Co., 1995.) This is a collection of poetry, homilies, and other varied ancient religious writings with one final section of modern Celtic poetry.

Davis, Courtney, and Gill Elaine. *The Book of Celtic Saints* (London: Blandford, 1995.) Courtney Davis is to be commended for her beautifully illustrated color drawings and Elaine Gill brings the stories of the Celtic saints to life in this splendid book. In addition each page is framed with a Celtic design. The chapter on Brigit notes that she is referred to as Ffraid Santes in Wales and in England and Scotland she is referred to as Saint Bride.

de Waal, Esther. *Every Earthly Blessing: Rediscovering the Celtic Tradition*. (Harrisburg, Penn.: Morehouse Publishing, 1999.) In this reissue of her older book, de Waal probes the inner spirit of Celtic spirituality as it is lived in the everyday lives of the people. She draws heavily on Carmichael and MacCleod. She deals also with its ties to Coptic and Syrian monasticism.

de Waal, Esther. *The Celtic Vision*. (Liguori, Mo.: Liguori/Triumph, 2002.) In this beautiful book of prayers covering themes such as creation, morning prayers, household prayers, saints and an-

Appendix 1

gels, Esther de Waal offers a treasure of prayers and blessings from the Outer Hebrides.

de Waal, Esther. *The Celtic Way of Prayer: The Recovery of the Religious Imagination.* (London: Hodder & Stoughton, 1996.) De Waal takes significant characteristics of Celtic spirituality and shows how they are reflected in poetry and prayer.

Donohoe, Ann. *Clonbroney with Ballinalee: A Local History.* (Longford: Ballinalee Guild, 1997.) This book provided some helpful information about Saint Samthann and connected the foundation at Clonbroney with Saint Patrick. The book also mentions that the National School is named after Saint Samthann.

Earle, Mary C. and Maddox, Sylvia. *Companions for the Journey: Praying with the Celtic Saints.* (Landover, Md.: Christian Brothers Publications, 2000.)

Earle, Mary C. and Maddox, Sylvia. *Praying with the Celtic Saints* (Winona, Minn.: St. Mary's Press, 1999) presents fifteen prayer companions who share the rich spirituality of Celtic Christianity with its sense of wonder, reverence for creation, love for the Trinity, and down-to-earth approach to life. The authors introduce the saints and legends associated with them and provide powerful prayer reflections that offer readers opportunities to integrate this rich Celtic heritage into their lives. This would be a great book for group discussion as well as personal prayer.

Eilis Ui Dhailigh, *Saint Gobnait of Ballyvourney.* (Ireland: Irish Messenger Publications, 1983.) A "classic" publication that recounts the story of Gobnait. This pamphlet was a primary source for our research on Gobnait and a treasure found at the local convenience story in Ballyvourney. Thanks is due to the author for capturing the legends of Gobnait for generations to come.

Ellis, Peter Berresford. *Celtic Women: Women in Celtic Society and Literature.* (Grand Rapids, Mich.: Wm. B. Eerdmans Publishing Co., 1996.) In this outstanding book, Peter Berresford Ellis concludes that early Celtic society was an egalitarian model, in which women could own property, divorce, govern, take prominent roles in political and religious life, even fight alongside men in battles. It was not until the arrival of the Roman and Germanic cultures and the arrival of Christianity that the rights of women began to disappear. This was a major resource for our research into the place of the *feminine* in Celtic society. Ellis's book, although scholarly, is highly readable.

Fewer, Michael. *The Beara Way*. (Dublin: Ordinance Survey, 2000.) This is a comprehensive traveler's guide for a tourist providing valuable background information about the Beara Peninsula in southwest Ireland. Detailed maps are provided and recommendations for walkers are included.

Fitzgerald, William John. *A Contemporary Celtic Prayer Book*. (Chicago: ACTA Publications, 1998.) Using a Liturgy-of-the-Hours format, Fitzgerald offers us prayers which immerse us in the Celtic spiritual mentality—a real help to interiorizing in prayer a Celtic mind-set. We recommend this inspiring book for individual and group prayer.

Green, Miranda. *Celtic Goddesses: Warriors, Virgins, and Mothers*. (London: The Bath Press, 1995.) Miranda Green, a scholar of Celtic myth, presents the beliefs and rituals associated with Celtic goddesses. The concept of partnership is prevalent in Celtic myth. Dr. Green presents evidence that some of the holy women and men of early Celtic Christian tradition resembled the pagan deities of earlier times. The pagan figures were absorbed in the Christian Church by transformation into saints.

Gill, Elaine and Everett, David. *Celtic Pilgrimages: Sites, Seasons, and Saints, An Inspiration for Spiritual Journeys*. (London: Blandford, 1997.) This fascinating book takes the reader on a pilgrimage to some of the places associated with Celtic saints. It takes armchair pilgrims on an inner spiritual journey to fifth-century double monasteries where women and men lived together in dedicated service of Christ. The illustrations draw you into the Celtic spirit.

Griffen, Toby D. *Celebrating the Celtic Saints*. (Springfield, Ill.: Templegate Publishers, 1998.) Griffen introduces us to male and female Celtic saints, including an appropriate symbol, scripture, meditation, and liturgical celebration for each.

Heaney, Marie. *Over Nine Waves: A Book of Irish Legends*. (London and Boston: Faber and Faber Ltd., 1994.) The author presents three Celtic mythic cycles in reader-friendly form, translating what often appears in other sources as complicated and erudite in a way that is entertaining and understandable to the average reader.

Hughes, Kathleen, and Hamlin, Ann. *The Modern Traveler to the Early Irish Church.* (Dublin: Four Courts Press, 1997.) The authors recreate the rich tradition of early ascetic sites, medieval parish churches, and monasteries. They provide a great list of early Christian sites county by county throughout Ireland which one can visit. They recommend that visitors to these sites get a large-scale map and watch out for nettles!

Jones, Noragh. *Power of Raven, Wisdom of Serpent.* (Edinburgh: Floris Books, 1994.) Women were the guardians of power and wisdom in the Celtic tradition. In this book, Noragh Jones describes the centuries-old rhythms of loving, birthing, mothering, healing, living and dying through the chants, rites, and traditions of life and spirituality. This book reminds us of the deep spiritual connection between all forms of life and the beautiful tapestry of prayer and blessing that Gaelic women wove through their lives. It is ideal for spiritual seekers who are looking for a book that echoes the experience of women as "hearth-keepers and life-givers."

Joyce, Timothy, O.S.B. *Celtic Christianity: A Sacred Tradition, A Vision of Hope.* (Maryknoll, N.Y.: Orbis Books, 1998.) In this volume Joyce contributes wonderful background material on the rise of Christianity, a unique, Celtic Christianity, in Ireland and other Celtic lands, and in demonstrating the effect of foreign strains on this particular style of Christianity. He includes material on the eastern influences on the Celtic church, and their channeling through Gaul; the position of women in the Celtic church, and the effects of various historical events on Celtic spirituality. He goes on to consider what threads of this spirituality may still endure, the present-day state of Christianity in Ireland, and among Irish immigrants to the United States, and the movement for a Celtic Renewal today. He mentions two relatively unknown female saints he discovered in traveling Ireland: Saint Ibar and Saint Surnaidhe whose church he discovered in Inishmor, and laments the ignoring of women's contributions by the many chroniclers of Irish religious history.

MacManus, Seamus. *The Story of the Irish Race: A Popular History of Ireland.* (New York: the Devin-Adair Company, 1944.) This book covers in a readable style the history and myth of ancient Ireland, and continues to trace historical events throughout its history through the treaty of 1914 and the establishment of the Irish Republic.

Maher, Mary. *Footsteps of Irish Saints.* (London: Burns Oates and Washbourne Ltd., 1926.) This book gives information on prominent Irish saints by diocese, including twenty-three dioceses and four archdioceses.

Newell, J. Philip. *The Book of Creation: An Introduction to Celtic Spirituality.* (Mahwah, N.J.: Paulist Press, 1999.) The author uses as his connecting theme the six days of Creation and the seventh day of rest in reflecting on the various characteristics of Celtic spirituality.

Newell, J. Philip. *Listening for the Heartbeat of God: A Celtic Spirituality.* (Mahwah, N.J.: Paulist Press, 1997.) Newell covers the integration of the pre-Christian and Christian in the development of Celtic Christianity, the influence of Pelagius and Eriugena in the shaping of the theological underpinnings of Celtic spirituality, and identifies the characteristics of Celtic spirituality.

O'Brien, Breege. "The Legacy of Saint Dymphna," a three-part article in *Muintir Acla: Achill Island Journal.* (Winter, 1999: 21–22; Spring, 1999: 39–40; Summer, 1999: 35–36.) This rich resource on the life and travels of Saint Dymphna synopsis for the reader much research into the legends and history of this controversial saint. Breege traces Dymphna from the kingdom of Oriel to Tydavnet in County Monaghan, to Lavey in County Cavan, then to Achill Island and eventually to Geel in Belgium, as the saint continuously fled the violent threats of her incestuous father. These articles and interviews with Breege and Sheila McHugh, also of Achill, provided information and insight into this courageous saint's legacy.

O'Connell, J. W., and Koriff, A. (eds). *The Book of the Burren.* (Kinvara, County Galway: Tir Eolas, 1991.) The editors provide a comprehensive guide to the stone monuments, wedge tombs, cashels, twelfth- to fifteenth-century churches, tower houses, and holy wells located in the wild stone landscape of the Burren. This book draws the reader into an exploration of the Burren as a sacred place. Before you begin a journey to holy wells in this area, this book will provide all the information you will need. A helpful map shows the location of forty-three holy wells in the Burren. Five of these wells are associated with Saint Innywee. Paddy Healy, a local farmer, led us to the well known for cure of warts. We visited Saint Brigit's Well in Liscannor. The water in this well falls gracefully over rock. The entrance to the well is an above-ground cave-like passage. The walls are surrounded with tokens, photos, articles of clothing, left by pilgrims. We felt a sense of peace and healing presence at this holy well.

O'Dwyer, Peter. *Towards a History of Irish Spirituality.* (Blackrock, County Dublin: The Columbia Press, 1995.) The author traces the influences on Celtic spirituality and on the Celtic Church, century by century.

O'Hogain, Dailhi. *The Sacred Isle: Belief and Religion in Pre-Christian Ireland.* (Wilton, Cork: The Collins Press, 1999.) This is an extensive presentation of the religious beliefs and practices in pre-Christian Ireland with insights into the importance of feminine deities and their Indo-European roots.

O'Maidin, Uinseann. *The Celtic Monk: Rules and Writings of Early Irish Monks.* (Spencer, Mass.: Cistercian Publications, 1996.) This collection of Celtic Rules of Life from various ancient monastic centers and of early writings provides insight into the inspiration and way of life of the Celtic mystics.

O'Riordain, John J. *Irish Catholic Spirituality.* (Mystic Conn.: Twenty-Third Publications, 1998.) John J. O'Riordain presents a thoughtful analysis of early Celtic influences in contemporary Irish spirituality and discusses the future of the church. He concludes: "When the church is seen as institution only, it is difficult for people on the margins who are more attuned to traditional faith-ways to maintain comfortable links with it. At her wise and generous best, the church has always been relaxed and generous about her boundaries."

O'Riordain, John J. *Saint Brigid of Ireland (Faughart) Pilgrim's Manual.* (Dundalk: Gene Lambe Printers, 2000.) (To obtain booklet call: 011-353-42-933-1781.) This booklet gives excellent background information about the beautiful shrine of Saint Brigid at Faughart. We were fortunate to have obtained this resource before our journey. It was this research and presentation which led us to include the "birthplace of Brigit" in our itinerary. There is also a reference to Saint Monenna as connected with Faughart as well as with Killeevy. He presents a series of "stations," an ancient Celtic prayer-form, in this handy guide as well.

Pemberton, Cintra. *Soulfaring: Celtic Pilgrimage Then and Now.* (Harrisburg, Penn.: Morehouse Publishing, 1999.) Sister Cintra, of the Order of Saint Helen, an Anglican Religious Congregation, has led numerous pilgrimages to Celtic religious sites, and creates for us an account of numerous holy shrines visited, details about these, and her own reflections on their impact for her life. This was a major help to us in planning our pilgrimage to ancient sites of holy women in Ireland and Wales. Her index in the back of the book for addresses and phone numbers proved quite valuable. Even if you could not physically go on a pilgrimage, you could be an "armchair" pilgrim and enrich your inner life by "traveling" *via* Centra's book.

Pullen, Bruce Reed. *Discovering Celtic Christianity: Its Roots, Relationships, and Relevance.* (Mystic, Conn.: Twenty-Third Publications, 1999.) This book combines the ancient Celtic Christian story with a modern pilgrimage. Join Bruce Pullen on a journey through Ireland and Wales where you visit the sites of saints like Brigid, Hilda, Kevin, Patrick, Ciarin, and Ninian. Find out how people today are inspired by ancient Celtic holy women and men. Each chapter contains a Scripture reflection and closing prayer.

Riain, Ide Ni. *Saint Ita.* (Dublin: Clonmore and Reynolds, Ltd. and London: Burns & Oates Ltd., 1964.) This little volume of 135 pages contains the many stories of Ita, and her sisters, Fiona and Nessa. The author consulted several ancient sources: *Vitae Sanctae Itae,* edited by Plummer from an ancient manuscript in the Bodleian Library, and the lives of several of her foster children: Saint Brendan and Saint Mochoemog, published by Plummer, and the life of Saint Fachtna and Cummene, and the *Felire* of Aengus the Culdee.

Roberts, Jack. *The Sacred Mythological Centres of Ireland: A Fully Illustrated Guide to the Ancient Ceremonial and Mythological Centres of the Landscape.* (Bandia Press, 1996.) This guidebook provides a splendid background of information and introduction to archaeological sites central to an understanding of Celtic antiquity and its feminine, goddess-orientation, in particular to the concept and primacy of the goddess of the land.

Sellner, Edward C. *Soulmaking: The Telling of a Spiritual Journey.* (Mystic, Conn.: Twenty-Third Publications, 1991.) Sellner narrates in journal-style his personal pilgrimage in search of the historical origins of the *anam chara* tradition.

Sellner, Edward C. *Wisdom of the Celtic Saints.* (Notre Dame, Ind.: Ave Maria Press, 1993.) Sellner covers the legends of numerous Celtic Saints, including several of the women, in a reader-friendly style. It proved to be a wonderful source for material on Saint Cannera and Saint Samthann. For a serious student of Celtic spirituality, it is a valuable resource.

Sheldrake, Philip. *Living Between Worlds: Place and Journey in Celtic Spirituality.* (Boston: Cowley Publications, 1996.) Sheldrake develops significant characteristics of the Celtic spiritual world-view.

Straffon, Cheryl. *The Earth Goddess: Celtic and Pagan Legacy of the Landscape.* (London: Blandford Book, 1997.) Ancient civilizations identify a female deity with earth, motherhood and nature. Recent archaeological research and interpretation of myth and legend rediscover the original earth-mother goddess of Ireland and Britain. This book gives a comprehensive country-by-country guide to the goddess sites in both countries. It includes an extensive list of *sheela-na-gigs,* including one in County Laois, at Culahull Castle, high up on the wall of the peel tower. However, it doesn't mention the one in Saint Gobnait's Church in Ballyvourney.

Walters, Johanna O'Mahony. *Tales of Travel and Trust: Our Celtic Heritage.* (Dublin: Veritas Publications, 1999.) This book is an excellent resource for presenting Celtic saints to children. It is beautifully illustrated and the legends are told in an imaginative, creative way. Highly recommended.

Wilde, Lyn Webster. *Celtic Women in Legend, Myth and History.* (London: Cassell, PLC, 1997.) In this book, Lyn Webster Wilde weaves together folklore, myth, historical record and archaeological evidence to provide a powerful view of Celtic women. There is a section on warrior women and myths such as Arianrhod, the Virgin Mother, replete with beautiful color illustrations and photos. A favorite shows the Beare Peninsula, home of the Hag of Beare. The last chapter includes a discussion on contemporary Celtic women who are working for the revival of language. In Scotland, women have carried on the poetic traditions because their walking songs have survived. The book includes photos of popular Celtic women musicians.

Woods, Richard J. *The Spirituality of the Celtic Saints.* (Maryknoll, N.Y.: Orbis Books, 2000.) Richard Woods, a Dominican theologian, presents a comprehensive overview of Celtic monasticism and its meaning for our times. He observes that "Samthann's reputation is that of a wise, even shrewd judge of character and a practical administrator...." He lists the places where Brigit was commemorated through the centuries: Ireland, Scotland, Wales, Portugal, Brittany, Cologne, Wurzburg, Paris, Constance, Maestricht, Mayence, Treve, and in parish churches from Italy to Iceland. Also, included are summaries of the lives of other Celtic holy women: Monenna, Cannera, and Gobnait. This book was an outstanding reference source for our research and one we highly recommend.

APPENDIX 2

Additional Resources for Celtic Sacred Journeys

Wales

Three outstanding guides to Celtic women sites are:

Noragh Jones
Troedrhiwsebon
Cwmrheidol
Aberystwyth
Sy23 3 NB
Wales
Phone: 011-44-1970-880-603
Co-Founder of Women Spirit Wales
E-mail: kennora@onetel.net.uk

Noragh took us on our sacred journey through Wales to the shrines and wells of the holy women we visited.

Ann Cowie
7 The Pebbles
Pembrokeshire
SA626RD
Wales, U.K.
"Trails through Wales"
St. David's Wales
011-44-1437-721-819

U. S. Address:
17716 Dominion Dr.
Sandy Spring, MD 20860
301-775-3227
E-mail: sarahcowiehere@yahoo.com

Ann provided stories and myths about ancient Celtic goddesses. She made arrangements for us to stay at Saint Non's Retreat Center, where Saint Non's chapel and well are located. This is a beautiful quiet place to stay. It overlooks Saint Bride's Bay and there are gorgeous walks around the area.

Nonna Rees
Treasury Cottage
Pembrokeshire
SA626RD
St. David's Wales, U.K.
011-44-1437-720-822

Nonna Rees, a librarian from Saint David's is also available to meet with groups. Nonna met with us and gave us a history of Saint Non and her shrine at Saint David's.

Accommodations

For information on places to stay in Wales, see the following:

Wales Tourist Board
551 Fifth Avenue
New York, New York 10176-0799
1-800-462-2748
E-mail: travelinfo@bta.org.uk

Saint Non's Retreat Center
St. David's, Wales

Saint Non's Retreat Center and Saint Winefride's Hospice: There is a beautiful chapel where people stop throughout the day for quiet prayer and meditation. Here also is Saint Non's Well. Contact the Welsh Tourist Board for other places to stay.

Saint Winefride:
Saint Winefride's Shrine and Well
Greenfield Valley Heritage Park
Holywell, Clwyd CH8 7QB, Wales
011-44-1352-714-172

On the day we visited we conducted interviews with Sister Margaret Reddy, Rev. Terence Carr, David Schwarz, Sr. Seraphim Boyce, and Sr. Laserian Fleming for our research for this book and a television program and video about Saint Winefride.

Saint Melangell:
Saint Melangell's Church
Pennant Melangell
North Powys
Mid Wales
Llangynog
Via Oswestry, SY10, OHQ Wales
011-44-1691-860-455

On the day we visited, we interviewed Rev. Evelyn Davies who shared many stories about the life of Saint Melangell and the history of this healing shrine.

Saint Tegla
Church of Saint Tegla and Saint Tegla's Holy Well
Llandegla
Wales
Church normally open 7:30 A.M.-6:00 P.M.

The people in the bed-and-breakfast accommodation next door to Saint Tegla's Church provided us with information about

Saint Tegla's Well and Church. We stayed in overnight in their lovely accommodations.

Ireland

For information on places to stay in Ireland, see the following:

Irish Tourist Board
Board Failte Eireann
345 Park Avenue
New York, NY 10154
1-800-223-6470
Web site: www.irelandvacations.ie

Saint Innywee's Church, the monastic ruins with the *sheela-na-gig*, is located at Killinaboy in the Burren, not far from Ennis, County Clare.

For more information, contact:

The Burren Center
Kilfenora, County Clare, Ireland
011-353-65-88030, fax 011-353-65-88102

Saint Brigit of Kildare: Sister Mary Minehan, a Brigidine sister, who does programs and retreats on Brigid and hosts groups from around the world at Solas Bhride Christian Community Center in Kildare, a place in which "all may experience community so that the spirit of Brigid may find appropriate expression in our time." After a gracious welcome, Sister Mary gave two interviews for a video and television program on Saint Brigit and took us on guided tours of Brigid's fire temple, church, and wells. On our visit in 2000, Sister Mary took us to an art exhibit where we met Gail Donovan, an artist from Adelaide, Australia, who has prepared beautiful illustrations on Saint Brigit's life. Visit Gail's Web site: gaildonovan.com and/or e-mail her at gail@gaildonovan.com.

To contact Saint Mary for a day of reflection or a tour, her e-mail address is *SolasBhride@eircom.net* or *solasbhride@tinet.ie*, or call Sister Mary or Sister Phil at 011-353-45-522-890 or write to Solas Bhride Community 14 Dara Park, Kildare, Ireland.

Saint Brigit's Shrine at Faughart and Saint Monenna's Well at Killeevy: Dolores Whelan, an educator and facilitator, gave an interview on Celtic spirituality and provided us with a guided tour of Saint Monenna's site at Killeevy in S. Armagh. To contact Dolores Whelan: e-mail: *journeys.irl@esatclear.ie* or call 011-353-42-937-190.

Saint Dymphna
Achill Island

Breege O'Brien, co-editor of *Muintir Acla, The Achill Island Journal* from 1995–1999 and author of "The Legacy of Saint Dymphna," a series of articles on Dymphna published in *Muintir Acla*, and Sheila McHugh who has a M.A. in Irish history and Masters of Theological Studies presented folklore and legends associated with Saint Dymphna. Breege gave a tour of Dymphna's site at Kildavnet on scenic Achill Island near the castle of the famous medieval pirate Grace O'Malley.

To contact Breege O'Brien: e-mail: *Breege@iegateway.net* or *bogoak@eircom.net* or call 011-353-98-4567. To contact Sheila McHugh: *e-mail: mchughs@eircom.net*.

Frank McCarron from Monaghan is a resident guide for Saint Dymphna's Church and Well in Tydavnet near Monaghan. Phone: 011-353-147-72543.

Ellie Sherry
Tirnasnoa, Tydavnet
County Monaghan, Ireland
011-353-047-89-583

Ellie was our guide who took us the hike across the fields to Saint Dymphna's Well in Tydavnet.

Bed and breakfast: We stayed with Mary McArdle on Clones Road, N 54. Phone: 011-047-82783.

Rev. Martin Treanor
Pastor of Saint Dymphna's Church
Tydavnet, County Monaghan

Father Martin gave permission to film paintings and mural of Saint Dymphna.

Rose Murray
Lavey, County Cavan

Saint Dymphna's Well is across from her home. She invited us in out of the rain and gave us a history of this beautiful well located down a steep embankment in the middle of a river.

Abbeylara, County Longford
For information about The Well of the Holy Women
Contact Mary E. Smyth
Toberphelan House

Mary has a wonderful bed and breakfast at a large Irish farm. We enjoyed the delicious food and warm hospitality.

Christina Lynch has a degree in Women's Studies. *The Well of the Holy Women* is located on her property.

Kilbride House
Abbyelara
County Longford
011-353-043-86094

For information about *Tobar Muire*, Mary's Well, and other holy wells in the Leenane area in Connemara, visit Michael O'Toole at Leenane Cultural Center, Leenane, Connemara, Ireland. Telephone: 011-353-95-42323/42231.

Mary's Shrine at Knock, Ireland
For information about Knock, County Mayo, Ireland
Telephone: 011-353-94-88100, fax 011-353-94-88295
E-mail: info@knock-shrine.ie
Visit Web site: http//www.knock-shrine.ie

For information about Old Clonbroney Cemetery, inquire at farm house adjacent to site, home of John, Mai, and Patricia O'Reilly, or e-mail them at *mareilly@gofree.indigo.ie*. This family graciously extended hospitality and resources to us regarding Saint Samthann's foundation originally at this site, although now inaccessible. Nothing remains but a cross standing on top of the wall of a cemetery.

Saint Gobnait: For information about the shrine and local celebrations, contact:

Margaret O'Connell
Ballyvourney, County Cork , Ireland
Telephone 011-353-26-45-054

If you are interested in finding out more about *sheela-na-gigs* and sacred space, visit Sila na Geige by Kathryn Price Theatana online: http://ourworld.compuserve.com/homepages/moonstone/Sheela.htm or send an e-mail to *moonstone@compuserve. com*.

Retreat Center: Myross Wood House
In 1999 we attended a Celtic program given by Rev. Michael Maher on Celtic spirituality. It was here we learned, according to the Irish perspective, that there is not a split between the earlier pagan and the later Christian tradition. Both are honored as the Sacred Story. Father Maher told us the story of the goddesses for whom Ireland is named and pointed us on the road to the "Paps of Anu," mountains near Killarney which are associated with an early mother goddess, Danu or Anu. For more information about retreats or programs, contact the director: Myross Wodd, Leap, County Cork. Telephone 011-353-2833118.

Cultural Recommendations

For a splendid Irish evening of entertainment, contact John and Rose Hallahan, directors of "A Taste of Ireland."

Thornhill House
Skibbereen,
County Cork, Ireland
Telephone 011-353-282-1387

For an unforgettable performance of the legends and myths of ancient Ireland, attend
Siamsa Tire Theatre
Tralee, County Kerry, Ireland
011-353-66-712-3055

For information on Bru Boru, a lively performances of Irish traditional song and dance at the Rock of Cashel, Tipperary, Ireland, e-mail: *bruboru@comhaltas.com*. This was one of the musical highlights of our trip in 1999.

Additional Resources for Celtic Studies/ Women's Spirituality Programs

To see video clips and photos from our spiritual travel, and to find information on future pilgrimages, retreats, and lectures, visit *www.godtalktv.org* or contact the authors at the following: *www.bridgetmarymeehan.com*.

Regina Madonna Oliver: e-mail: Loris@intercom.net
Bridget Mary Meehan: e-mail: sofiabmm@aol.com
Celtic videos now available from www.godtalktv.org

In *Quest of the Celtic Soul*, a one-hour video leads the viewer to encounter "thin places" sacred to the Irish where the veil between past, present, and future is nearly transparent, you will contemplate the lives of amazing fifth-century holy women such as Brigit of Kildare, Ita of Killeedy, Cannera of Bantry Bay, and Gobnait of Ballyvourney who lived their vision and continue to inspire through the ages and in every generation. Video includes prayers and questions for discussion and reflection.

Discovering the Sacred Feminine in Celtic Mythology: In this video, Noragh Jones, founder of Woman-Spirit Wales and Ann Cowie from "Trails thru Wales," share delightful myths and legends of the feminine divine in the Gaelic traditions. In a deep way, stories like the Hag of Beara, teach us to laugh and play and discover our true wisdom as we age. Warrior women like Macha, Maeve, Morrigu, and Arianrod, challenge us to speak truth to power, and to champion equality and justice in our world. Images such as The Three-in-One, Virgin, Mother and Crone, and *sheela-na-gigs,* ancient fertility symbols birth us into wholeness and harmony with our universe.

Saint Winefride of Holywell, Wales: A Wounded Healer. Saint Winefride's shrine in North Wales has been a popular place of pilgrimage since the seventh century and the only shrine in Britain that has an unbroken history of pilgrimage to the present day. In this program the spiritual leaders from Holywell explore the ancient heritage of this sacred shrine and Celtic princess saint and share stories of powerful healings that have occurred in recent years.

Saint Brigit of Kildare: Ablaze with God's Womb-Compassion. Some commentators believe that Saint Brigit heard confessions, celebrated Mass, and ordained clergy. This video includes interviews with Sister Mary Minehan from Kildare and Dolores Whelan from Dundalk, Ireland. There is powerful artwork depicting Brigit as a woman for the millennium by Gail Donovan from Adelaide, Australia. It also takes viewers to Brigit's wells and features footage of beautiful stained-glass windows including one depicting her ordination as bishop!

If you are interested in finding out more about Celtic videos go to the Web site: *www.godtalktv.org* or e-mail Bridget at *sofiabmm@aol.com*.

Recipes

Irish Soda Bread or Scones

1 lb. (3-1/2 cups) flour
1 teaspoon salt
1 teaspoon bicarbonate of soda
1 teaspoon sugar (optional)
1 pint buttermilk

Mix the dry ingredients well together. Make a well in the middle of the flour. Pour in most of the buttermilk mixing the flour from the sides. Do not let the mixture get too dry.

Turn onto a floured board. Knead gently until smooth. Make a cross on top. Place in a floured cake tin. Bake in oven at 425° F or 218° C for approximately 45 minutes. To test if done, tap the base of the cake. If it sounds hollow, it is ready.

(For scones, add raisins to dry ingredients; make the same way, and roll out in scone shapes.)

Brown Bread

4 cups stoneground, wholemeal, coarse whole wheat flour
1 cup white flour
1 tablespoon and 1 teaspoon bran
1 tablespoon wheat germ
1 level teaspoon bicarbonate of soda
1 teaspoon salt
1 egg
15 ozs. buttermilk
2 tablespoons sunflower or flora oil

Mix all dry ingredient together. Add egg and oil. Grease a loaf tin. Bake for one hour at 400° F. or 200° C.

(FROM NOREEN DAVY, COUSIN OF BRIDGET MARY MEEHAN)

a Circle Dance

DANCE LITURGY

In recent years the labyrinth has gained popularity, and "walking the labyrinth" as a spiritual exercise has undergone a resurrection in the Christian West. Modeled on the famous labyrinth in the Chartres Cathedral, and on several similar mazes in Ireland, churches in the United States have brought in temporary designs on gigantic canvases, or have built outdoor labyrinthian walkways to foster the prayer-walk and its meditative richness.

This prayer-walk (into the center along a circular pathway, with a meditative pause in the central "eye," followed by the winding-walk outwards) has been heralded as a way to insight and enlightenment. It *enacts* our walk through life and life's uncertainties, allowing body and mind to join together participating in a unified prayer-experience. In some respects it is not unlike the pilgrimage or the procession, except that the procession is always a communal walk, whereas the pilgrimage and the labyrinth-walk may be done either individually or in the company of others.

The religious circle dance is within this category of life-walk dramatizations! It is done in the company of others. In fact, it cannot be danced without the collaboration of a sufficient number of participants to create a functional dance circle! It adds to the walking experience a cultural musical accompaniment, and demands the matching of body rhythm to the rhythm of music (which is, in turn, a reflection of the natural rhythms of the created universe).

In the Celtic world, everything was integrated: medicine, astronomy, spirituality, and the natural world. Our generation in the West is rediscovering the interconnectedness of the created universe, and is re-evaluating the importance of the communal as a counterbalance to isolation.

Circle dancing integrates voice, movement, energy, and concentration, and counteracts isolation. The circle symbolizes the beginning and the end, *alpha* and *omega*, as well as the unending-ness of God and an *eternal life*. Just as the circular symbol around the Celtic cross speaks subliminally of the earth as our home, of the womb-source of our being, of the sun's orb as our energy source, of the ever-seeing eye of God, and of the surrounding embrace of a loving God, so the circle of the dance carries these connotations to the intuitive heart of the participant.

To celebrate communally our growing awareness of the Celtic life-vision, and of our common and communal search for God as a personal and embracing Presence in our lives, let us dance this Circle Dance as our closing prayer.

The Dance Pattern

1. With others of the group, form a circle, holding hands. Raise the hands to form little peaks. *One person* is designated the *leader*; but this *leader*, at the beginning of the dance, is part of the circle.

2. The music may be a Celtic jig, or appropriate Irish music in speedy 4/4 time or 2/4 time. The important objective for all participants is to *continue holding hands, and moving with the group, no matter where the leader leads!*

3. In a circle, holding hands all around, with arms lifted so the joined hands form little "peaks," and following the leader's guidance:

   a. Turn toward the left and walk 16 steps to the left, *stamping* on number 16.

   b. Turn to the right and walk 16 steps to the right, ending with *stamp, stamp* on the fifteenth and sixteenth steps.

   c. The leader drops his/her left hand, letting loose of the connection. (Now there is a line of dancers which is circular.)

   d. The leader turns to the left and begins to spiral inwards, making his/her end of the line of dancers follow her as she winds inwards in an increasingly ever-smaller circle, as he/she moves toward the center. (The movement, according to Celtic tradition, is "clockwise," or "sun-wise," the direction of the "blessing.")

   e. Once in the center, the leader makes a decisive turn to the *left* (totally opposite to the direction he/she has been moving) and begins the spiraling march outwards. All the participants have to do is keep hands joined and follow the leader in rhythm to the music. The *leader* has the challenge to keep her/his head, and continue to spiral outwards without getting confused in passing those who are still moving "inwards."

   f. The outwards spiral continues until the entire line is completely back in a large circle. It is up to the leader, once the circle is "unwound," to once again *turn right* (so the dancers may come together in a circle facing one another, instead of back to back.

g. Once the circle is back in shape, the leader joins hands with the last person in the line, once again creating the joined dance circle.

h. Then, turning toward the left, he/she leads the circle in 16 steps to the left, with a *stamp* on the sixteenth. Then, turning toward the right, she leads the circle sixteen steps to the right, with *stamp*, *stamp* on the fifteenth and sixteenth steps. The dance is over!

Weaving the Brigit Cross

A Traditional Celtic Prayer

> *Cross, cross, Brigit and her cross!*
> *Mary and her Son;*
> *Brigit and her cloak,*
> *Good as we are today,*
> *May we be seven times better*
> *A year from now!*

1. For each cross one needs 16 or 20 lengths of supple reed (or narrow palm fronds, or supple willow shards), either 10 inches or 12 inches long. (The number of lengths will determine the number of rows of *weave* at the center; the number of inches will determine the dimension of the arms of the cross.)

2. Have on hand a roll of transparent tape, to help secure your work as you weave and make the problem of holding the woven center together less difficult. Have ready four bag-ties to use in gathering the fronds together at the tips of each quadrant of the cross.

3. For each cross you need one (1) extra length of reed, preferably one more rigid than the others' lengths. This will serve as an *anchor*, and finding its center, you *weave* the more *supple fronds* around it. (Sometimes, to make the weaving fronds supple enough for the weaving process, they need to be soaked in water overnight!)

4. Fold the supple fronds in half.

5. Place frond #1 over the *anchoring stiff frond* with one leg on one side of it, and the other on the opposite. Draw it nearly to the center, but leave a little space because frond # 4 will have to be *threaded through it*, as though through the eye of a needle.

6. Place frond #2 at a right angle to the first frond, on the other side of the *anchor*. Place one *leg* of it on the upper outside, and the other *leg* on the lower outside.

7. Place frond #3 at a right angle to the legs of frond. #2. Bring one of its *legs* over the top of frond 2 and the *anchor*. Bring the other *leg* under the under-leg of frond #2 and the *anchor*.

8. Now, place frond #4 in the last quadrant at a right angle #3. Then have the two legs of frond #4 thread through the *eye of frond #1*, and tighten all fronds towards the center. They will form a braided square around the anchor frond.

9. Lay out the next four fronds which have been folded in half. They are #5, #6, #7, and #8.

10. Place frond #5 to the outside edge of frond #1, with the two legs straddling the *anchor*.

11. At a right angle to #5, place #6 with each of its legs on either side of frond #4.

12. Place #7 at a right angle to #6. Have its two legs straddle both #6 and the *anchor frond*.

13. Place #8 at a right angle to #7. Have its two legs straddle #7, and thread them through the eye at the bent end of #5. Draw all four fronds towards the center for a second woven row, adding to the square effect around the center of the *anchor*.

14. Follow these steps for 9 through 12 for the next four fronds, #9, 10, 11, 12; and then, again for the nest of four: #13, 14, 15, 16. (This will give four [4] woven rows forming a square around the *anchor* at its center.)

15. To hold the woven fronds at the center, a small piece of transparent tape can be attached to the underside of the central woven square.

16. The open legs of the fronds will now extend in four directions. They should be gathered at each of the four tips and fastened by a bag-tie to form the four arms of the Brigit Cross. This cross is prominent in Irish homes, calling for God's peace and protection on the family.